Training the Church of the Future

Auburn Seminary Lectures on
Christian Nurture with Special
Reference to the Young People's
Society of Christian Endeavor as a

Training - School of the Church

by

Rev. Francis E. Clark, D.D.

First Fruits Press
Wilmore, Kentucky
c2015

Training the church of the future: Auburn Seminary lectures on Christian nurture with special references to the Young People's Society of Christian Endeavor as a training-school of the church, by Rev. Francis E. Clark.

First Fruits Press, ©2015
Previously published: New York and London : Funk & Wagnalls Company, ©1902.

ISBN: 9781621713418 (print), 9781621713425 (digital)

Digital version at http://place.asburyseminary.edu/christianendeavorbooks/3/

Clark, Francis E. (Francis Edward), 1851-1927.
      Training the church of the future : Auburn Seminary lectures on Christian nurture with special references to the Young People's Society of Christian Endeavor as a training-school of the church [electronic resource] / by Rev. Francis E. Clark.
      225 pages ; 21 cm.
      Wilmore, Ky. : First Fruits Press, ©2015.
      Reprint. Previously published: New York ; London : Funk & Wagnalls Company, ©1902.
      ISBN: 9781621713418 (pbk.)
      1. Religious education. 2. International Society of Christian Endeavor.. I. Title.
BV1425 .C6 2015

Cover design by Jonathan Ramsay

asburyseminary.edu
800.2ASBURY
204 North Lexington Avenue
Wilmore, Kentucky 40390

First Fruits
THE ACADEMIC OPEN PRESS OF ASBURY SEMINARY

First Fruits Press
The Academic Open Press of Asbury Theological Seminary
204 N. Lexington Ave., Wilmore, KY 40390
859-858-2236
first.fruits@asburyseminary.edu
asbury.to/firstfruits

Training the Church of the Future

WILLISTON CHURCH, PORTLAND, ME.
(In this Church the First Christian Endeavor Society Was Formed)

3

Training the Church of the Future

Auburn Seminary Lectures on Christian Nurture
with Special Reference to the
Young People's Society of Christian Endeavor
as a
Training-School of the Church

BY

Rev. FRANCIS E. CLARK, D.D.

Founder of the Young People's Society of Christian Endeavor. Author of
" The Children and the Church," " Young People's Prayer-Meetings,"
" The Great Secret," " A New Way Around an Old
World," Etc., Etc.

NEW YORK AND LONDON

FUNK & WAGNALLS COMPANY

1902

4

5

To

the Young Pastors of the Country, to the Young
Men in the Theological Seminaries, and to All who
are engaged in Practical Christian Work within
the Church, this volume is inscribed in the
hope that in it they may find some
suggestions for Training the
Church of the Future.

TABLE OF CONTENTS

BY WAY OF INTRODUCTION

THE volume which is herewith presented to the public is the result of a suggestion made by the President and faculty of Auburn Theological Seminary, that I should prepare a course of lectures on Christian Nurture with especial reference to the Society of Christian Endeavor as a means of Christian training.

Much has been written on this subject, but never to my knowledge has there been a systematic effort to set forth the great principles of Christian nurture as they are related to the modern young people's movement. However imperfectly I have succeeded, this volume is an attempt in this direction. Much new light has been thrown upon child nature by recent studies in psychology that tend to establish the principles which in a practical way have been confirmed by the experience of a multitude of busy pastors during the past twenty years.

These lectures were delivered first at Auburn, then at Oberlin, and afterward in an abbreviated form at the Congregational Seminary of Chicago, at McCormick Seminary of the latter city, and also in the schools of the prophets at Andover, Bangor, Newton, Rochester, New Brunswick, and in the Union Seminary of New York.

By Way of Introduction

They have often been received by faculty and students with a favor which I felt was beyond their desert, but which, however undeserved, has encouraged me to accept the further suggestion of the President of Auburn Seminary, and prepare them for publication with the hope that in their printed form they may still accomplish something for the advancement of the Kingdom among the young.

In the Appendix will be found much information concerning the Young People's Society of Christian Endeavor and its later developments, which has not before been brought together within the covers of one book. This method of Christian nurture seems to be receiving the renewed and continual blessing of God. Nearly four millions of young people are being trained in such schools of Applied Christianity, and millions more have graduated therefrom. The Society is constantly growing in numbers, and I believe in spiritual grace, in America and in every other land. It will soon be twenty-one years old, and as this society "comes of age" and enters upon its years of strength and maturity, I would ask the prayers of every reader of this book that it may in the years to come modestly, efficiently, and more fully than in the past, prove a training-school for the Church of the Future.   FRANCIS E. CLARK.

BOSTON, MASS., December, 1901

THE CHURCH OF THE FUTURE

TRAINING

THE

CHURCH OF THE FUTURE

Chapter I

THE CHURCH OF THE FUTURE

THE PROBLEM BEFORE US—ITS IMPORTANCE AND VALUE—THE STANDPOINT OF THE AUTHOR—WHERE IS THE CHURCH OF THE FUTURE?—THE IDEA OF CONQUEST AND THE IDEA OF GROWTH—NO ANTAGONISM BETWEEN THE TWO—CHRISTIAN NURTURE DOES NOT PRECLUDE CHILD CONVERSION—THE IMPORTANCE OF THE STUDY—DIFFERENT TYPES OF CONVERSION—AN APPEAL TO PERSONAL EXPERIENCE—ADOLESCENCE A MOST CRITICAL PERIOD—"THE APPETITE FOR THE INFINITE"—THE DIFFICULTIES IN THE WAY OF CHRISTIAN NURTURE—"THE TYRANNY OF THE PUBLIC SCHOOL"—THE VIEW OF THE PSYCHOLOGISTS—OBSTACLES, THINGS TO BE OVERCOME—SERMON-STEEPED SAINTS AND SERMON-HARDENED SINNERS—HOW MUCH TIME SHOULD BE GIVEN TO CHRISTIAN NURTURE—THE LIFE-INSURANCE SYSTEM OF AVERAGES—TESTIMONIES FROM EMINENT MEN—EARLY CONVERSION OF NOTABLE CHRISTIANS—DO EARLY CHURCHGOING HABITS CREATE A DISTASTE FOR RELIGION?—THE COLLECTED OPINIONS OF MANY REPRESENTATIVE CHRISTIANS—"THE CHILDREN WHOM THOU HAST GIVEN ME."

THE great problem before us is the upbuilding of the Kingdom of Christ. It is not primarily the advocacy of a society or a method or a plan of work. It is not simply the Christian nurture of the young, but it is the

13

Training the Church of the Future

Christian nurture of the young *with a purpose*—for the sake of the Kingdom.

The subject of our study is as important as the church itself, for upon it the future of the church depends. It is as essential as the study of theology, of church history, of exegesis, for its object and purpose are the very same: to find out how, through these studies, one may be fitted to extend the Kingdom of Jesus Christ and strengthen His church on earth. If the suggestions that I make prove of any value, it will not be that I speak with eloquence, originality, or authority, but because I shall speak from the standpoint of actual practise. I shall look at these matters with a pastor's eye, remembering at every point my own pastoral experience. I shall look at them from the standpoint of a worker who has spent all his years among the young, who believes in young people, who trusts young people, who expects great things from young people, and whose expectations have rarely been disappointed. We are to consider The Training of the Church of the Future.

First, then, it is important to know what the Church of the Future is and where it is. The answer is obvious. The Church of the Future is in the nurseries and schoolhouses, in the colleges and the shops and factories, and on the playgrounds of the present. The children and youth of to-day are the Church of the Future. There are two ways of building up the Kingdom of God: first, the method of conquest; second, the method of growth.

14

The Church of the Future

Sometimes the church has laid stress on one method, sometimes on the other. Sometimes it has won its victories from without, sometimes from within. Sometimes emphasis has been put upon revival methods—the widespread awakening, the winning of men hardened in sin and cased in indifference and worldliness. At other times the pendulum has swung to the other extreme, and the sole emphasis has been laid upon the method of growth; growth among the children of the church, in the households of communicants. But the history of the church proves that neither method is sufficient by itself, and that neither excludes the other.

During the last century and the early half of this century in many Protestant churches the emphasis was placed upon the idea of conquest. Wide, sweeping revivals marked the history of the church. Wonderful scenes, often attended with extravagant and grotesque manifestations, were of frequent occurrence. Sermons that stirred men to the very foundations of their being were preached by Edwards and his contemporaries. Whitefield, Finney, Nettleton, and men of their stamp added vast numbers to the church—captives taken, as it were, in the stress and storm of war.

With the advent of Bushnell and his theories, the attention of the church was called, as never before, to the supreme importance of Christian nurture, and it was seen that, whatever the conquest might be from without, there must also be growth from within if the church was to hold its own and retain the allegiance and loyalty of those who naturally belonged to it.

With the development of this idea the church naturally set itself to devise new and more effective methods of winning and training the young for herself. Many Sunday-schools became not simply agents for *instructing* the children and youth, but more and more *evangelistic* agencies. Young people's societies were multiplied; pastor's classes were formed. This burden was laid ever more heavily upon the hearts of pastors and people alike: "How shall we win and train our youth before they wander into the highways of sin?" "How shall we make the children *of* the church, children *in* the church?"

Surely if only one method could be used, either that of conquest or growth, the results obtained from growth would be vastly greater than the difficult and uncertain fruits of conquest over the indifferent or vicious. But we are not shut up to one method; the two are needed, each to supplement the other. There will always be hardened men, men steeped in sin who have passed beyond the period of Christian nurture and who must be won, if they are won at all, by the more apparently forceful and startling methods of the evangelist. It has been truly said by a modern philosophic writer: "What education and discipline do slowly, painfully, and doubtfully in fitting the soul for the common life, is often done at a single stride by the fiery enthusiasm of religious passion, and the victims of inverted education and

16

The Church of the Future

fatal opportunities are wrenched in an instant from the
habits of one or even two decades and become most valuable ministers of the common needs."*

At the same time, all history proves that at the best
but a small fraction of men are reached with the gospel
message after they have passed the period of youth and
young manhood. At the most the method of conquest
will win but a comparative few. The great majority,
if they are saved for the church at all, must be saved by
other methods; by the slow, careful, and often impercep-
tible processes of Christian growth and training. "The
Lord hath set up churches," quaintly says Cotton Mather,
"only that a few old Christians may keep one another
warm while they live, and then carry away the church
with them when they die? No, but that they might with
all care nurse still successively another generation of
subjects to our Lord, that they may stand up in His
Kingdom when they are gone."†

Yet it is not altogether fair thus to separate these two
methods of building up the Kingdom—growth and conquest. Even in the youngest heart there is conquest, as
well as growth; in the oldest and most hardened there
must be growth after the period of conquest. The difference of method seems to be greater than it really is.
Because it is comparatively easy for the young heart to
yield to the influence of the Spirit, nevertheless yield it

---

* Granger, " The Soul of a Christian." p. 60.
† Cotton Mather, " Magnalia," Book I.

must and does before it enters into the Kingdom. Because it is so much easier to bend the twig than the full-grown tree, this does not prove that it is not necessary to bend the twig.

Nothing that I may say in regard to Christian nurture or child training precludes in my mind the necessity of child conversion. The process of conversion may be a very gentle and simple one. The child may never know the exact moment of the turn in his pathway. But some time the turn was made, some time he made the choice, and, tho there was no wrench of old habits, no upheaval of the old nature, no earthquake shock or tornado of passion, his whole future life, if he has indeed entered into the Kingdom, proves that there was a choice that placed him among the children of God. What a fascinating study is this, and what a soul-absorbing task, that a pastor shall seek with all the skill and all the resources and all the holy art of which he is master, to lead out the soul of the child and the youth into the large place of spiritual vision and activity which God meant it to occupy! As President G. Stanley Hall says in his lecture on the religious conquest of the child's mind:

"Childhood is the very best period of human life. Then all human faculties are at their best. It is the paradise from which growth is always more or less of a fall. . . . In all its activities, physiological and psychical, the child is nearer the type of the species and has less of the limitations of the individual. The doors of

18

the prison-house have closed upon him far less tightly than they have upon us."

But not only is this the most interesting period of life to deal with, it is one that requires and repays the most careful study. It demands the finest appreciation of the period we have to work upon and the most careful adaptation of all our means to the supreme end to be accomplished—the end of revealing God and the spiritual world to the young soul, and of establishing him in his faith in unseen realities.

"Why should not the care of souls become an art," says Professor Coe in his valuable book on "The Spiritual Life," "a system of organized and proportioned methods based upon definite knowledge of the material to be wrought upon, the ends to be obtained, and the means and instruments of obtaining them. Such an art would require scientific insight into the general organization of the mind and especially into the particular characteristics of the child mind, the youth mind, and the mature mind. . . . The religious artist will study when and how and how far to administer instruction to the intellect, incitement to the feeling, and stimulus to the will. . . . Many a revival worker is equipped with texts and advice and exhortation, all neatly classified and ready for application; but the investigation of the cases is utterly superficial and no connection is ordinarily established between the remedy and the difficulty. Of course some will say that the method approves itself by its results, but the same may be said of patent medicine. After all, the question is not merely whether we get results, but, rather, do we get the best results and the most of them? For this knowledge is as necessary in the cure of souls as in the healing of bodies."

Our ideas concerning conversion have been confused sometimes because we have confined ourselves to a single type. The story of the conversion of St. Paul dominated the Church for hundreds of years, but there was only one St. Paul; while there were a multitude in the early Church apparently, who came into the Kingdom as did Peter and Andrew and James and John; and a multitude more undoubtedly, who, like the young Timothy, could trace the beginning of their Christian lives to a grand-mother Lois or a mother Eunice.

In these lectures I shall speak largely of the Timothy type of conversion. That there is such a type, well recognized and distinct, is shown not only by the Bible, but by the history of the Church. It is a happy thing, indeed, and augurs well for the future, that the Church has come to recognize this as a normal, healthy, natural type, and that she is seeking to build herself up in these days quite as much by growth from within as by conquest from without.

That Christian nurture is a God-given way of building up the Church, and perhaps the chief way that He has ordained, is shown by facts which all religious history must recognize: First, the capacity of the young to receive Christ into their hearts. I confidently appeal to the personal experience of many who read these words to verify this statement. Is it not true that as children, quite as much as in later years, your hearts were opened to divine things? Did you not hear the still, small voice? Was not the presence of God a very real thing when you were eight or ten or twelve years of age? Could you not appreciate something of the love of Christ and His sacrifice for you? Did not your little heart burn with good impulses to serve Him with all a child's might? You may have forgotten these early days, and sometimes the experiences may seem very dim and unreal to you, but I think there are few Christian men who have not some remembrance of these things? Indeed, I venture to say that many of you date your first strivings and resolves to be Christians back to tender years, and you will bear me witness that divine things were real and substantial matters of your every-day life in your earlier childhood.

I am not speaking of prodigies and precocious hot-house human plants, but of every-day, rough-and-ready, noisy, natural boys. If you were brought up in a Christian home, if you read your Bible and prayed at your mother's knee, it was as natural to be a member of the family of God as to be a member of your father's household. To be sure, there doubtless came a period later when companion and school, when passion and fashion had their influence, and these early religious aspirations and thoughts were dimmed and dulled; but the earliest experiences to which I refer prove the capacity of the child to be a disciple.

21

The very fact that so large a proportion of present church-members turned to God in their early years, proves beyond question the capacity of the young heart for divine things, and puts a tremendous importance upon the matter of youthful training for God. I have spoken of the large place of spiritual vision and activity which God has prepared for the soul of man. It is peculiarly interesting to note what modern psychologists have demonstrated: that there is an age when God peculiarly opens the doors of the spiritual world to the eager soul, and that is the period of adolescence with which we in these lectures have particularly to do—the period between childhood and maturity, between boyhood and manhood, between girlhood and womanhood; the "place where the brook and river meet."

"Adolescence," says Professor Starbuck, "is one of the most critical periods of development, a time when the youth should be treated with the utmost delicacy and discretion. It is the point toward which all the lines of tendency during childhood converge and interplay with racial forces to determine the direction of the later development. It is the point at which the blunder may prove most fatal, and that likewise in which wisdom and discretion can reap the greatest harvest."*

Professor Coe in his studies confirms the same view.

"During the next three or four years [after the age of twelve]," he says, "there is to come a transformation of the mental as well as of the physical organism, more

* Starbuck, "Psychology of Religion."

22

profound than any other between birth and death. New kinds of sensations and emotions, new modes of thought, new attitudes of will, new meanings of life, new problems of duty, new kinds of temptation, new mysteries of religion, all these come in a flood over the young adolescent. . . . If there be a heavenly Father who yearns for fellowship with His children, what more effective method could there be of satisfying that yearning than to attach to adolescence an appetite for the Infinite, the infinitely true, beautiful, and good. As a matter of fact such an appetite for the Infinite is just the most characteristic part of mental adolescence." *

With these thoughts in mind of the critical nature of the period of adolescence and its wonderful possibilities for good and ill, we may well emphasize and underscore what Professor Coe says on a later page.

"He who aspires to be a pastor should doubtless aim to understand and sympathize with the religious difficulties of persons of all ages. It would be entirely in place to enter a plea for the understanding of childhood or of mature life or of old age, but all these are being better understood and cared for than the remaining period of life, that of adolescence. . . . Stiff-necked and obstinately self-contained toward all attempts to drive or force it, the heart of youth is nevertheless more docile than the heart of a child toward one who understands it and is willing to impart to it the guidance that it so sorely needs." *

If the importance of the period of adolescence is so

* Coe, " The Spiritual Life."

vast to the individual himself, it follows that its importance to the church is no less great. "The thoughts of youth are long, long thoughts," and the impressions that are made upon the heart in the period of adolescence are abiding and stedfast. Then the clay can be molded, to be sure, but it "*sets*" very rapidly, and often forever. In this is found the reason for the undoubted fact that the stedfastness of young converts is quite as great as of those who have come into the church in later years. In fact, I believe that of those who have been true to their first love the proportion is far larger among the converts whose hearts were mastered by love in early years.

How many drunkards who give up their cups in middle life remain stedfast to their pledge? Some say, one in a hundred; some say, one in ten; others give more cheering figures; but the proportion of reformed drunkards who lose their grip and go back to their cups is startlingly large. So is the proportion of those persons who profess conversion in mature years. Many remain stedfast and are shining examples of the grace of God, and their later activity is all the more marked because of their early indifference; but among the converts of middle and later life are many others who lapse again into worldliness, carelessness, and indifference, and whose fruit is not the "fruit of the Spirit," but the "apples of Sodom."

"If it was not true of Paul," says Bushnell, "it is yet

too generally true that one born out of due time will be found out of due time more often than he should be afterward—unequal, inconsistent with himself, acting the old man instead of the new. Having the old habit to war with, it is often too strong for him. To make a graceful and complete Christian character it needs itself to be the habit of existence, not a grape grafted on a bramble."*

What I have already said implies what I believe is absolutely true, that those who are most active and earnest in the church to-day are those who were early converted. With many brilliant exceptions to this rule, the rule nevertheless holds true. Again and again the test has been made, and again and again it has been found that the working force of the church to-day received its first impulse to the religious life in very early years. Then all these facts combined: the capacity of the young readily to receive Christ, the fact that the great majority of those who become Christians at all become so in early life, the comparative stedfastness of young Christians in mature years, the larger proportion of earnestness and activity that they show, and the correlative fact of the comparative hopelessness of middle age and old age, make this problem perhaps the most serious and pressing that can engage the attention of Christian workers.

I confess I see few matters of such vast importance as

* Bushnell, "Christian Nurture."

this within all the range of theologic training; few questions so imperative and pressing upon the Church of to-
day as the question of Christian nurture. The very life
of the Church depends upon it; the existence of the in-
stitutions for which the Church stands. The problem
whether or not she is to be the saving salt of the future
generations, or whether they shall drop into decay because the salt has lost its savor, depends upon whether
we shall bring the children to Christ and train them for
His service; whether our sons shall grow up as tender
plants and our daughters be fashioned after the simili-
tude of a palace.

We must not suppose, however, because the child nature is accessible and easily molded that therefore there
are no obstacles or difficulties in the way, and that
persistent and earnest effort is not needed. There are
very serious obstacles to the conversion of the young and
to their Christian training—difficulties peculiar to youth
which often require all a loving pastor's care and ingenuity to overcome. The young are peculiarly susceptible
to the influence of their surroundings. Indifference and
coldness chill them more quickly than their elders.
More intuitively than older persons do they distinguish
between those who are really interested in their welfare
and those who simulate such an interest for professional
or other reasons. They are sensitive, too, in an unusual
degree to the spiritual condition of the home and the
church. In a warm, active, evangelistic church, the

young people will keep up with their elders, if they do not surpass them in activity. In an indifferent and formal church, whatever the wealth lavished upon architecture and fittings, however eloquent the preaching or tuneful the choir, the young life will not level up to the architecture or the eloquence, but will level down to the indifference of the Christians in the pews. There is no better thermometer to the real spiritual life of a church than its young people's work. From the children of the home you can judge—not infallibly, but with a great degree of certainty—of the character of the home. From the children of the church you can judge still more certainly of the character of the church. It must be confessed that the trend of the times is not altogether favorable to the Christian nurture of the young. To be "pious" is not "good form" in many communities—in our colleges in particular. Many young people hear the Bible criticized oftener than they hear its teachings commended to the conscience. There is a certain kind of preaching all too prevalent that feeds the intellect but not the heart. This is as fatal to Christian nurture as it is to the truest spiritual graces of older people.

There is also to be reckoned with in the present day an overweening pride of intellect, which makes the Christian life of young people more difficult than it was fifty years ago or even ten years ago.

The "tyranny of the public school," as it is called, has gained and is gaining force, and to speak a word against its undue intrusion into the family and church life of the day almost relegates one to the ranks of uncultured antediluvians. Many young people are so busy with their arithmetic or their Latin grammar that they have time for but a brief glance at their Bibles, and that often is given only on Sunday. It is an unpardonable sin to be tardy at school. To be absent a whole day is a crime in the minds of many children that ranks with an infraction of the decalog, even if it does not take precedence of at least the fourth or fifth commandment. This is really a question of very serious consideration and worthy of prolonged thought, prayer, and discussion—are we not purchasing at too great a cost the intellectual equipment, such as it is, of the rising generation?

Many parents take the ground: "My children are in school. This is their intellectual harvest-time. Nothing must be allowed to interfere with their studies—at least no religious meetings must interfere, but of course the party and the social engagement may be excepted." The young people's meeting has often been moved, sometimes to its detriment, from a week evening to Sunday evening, and crowded into a brief and interrupted half-hour before the second service. The midweek prayer-meeting is out of the question for many young people because of their parents' strict prohibition. The second service of Sunday keeps them up too late for their lessons on Monday morning, so they are not allowed to attend it. Or it is thought that the poor little tender blossoms will wilt and die if they are expected to attend two or three services on Sunday, tho five hours a day for five days in the week, with plenty of home study for the spare hours, is not thought too much for the Moloch of public opinion to demand from the schools. I am not speaking of worldly parents who are utterly indifferent to the religious motive. These things you might expect of such. But many Christian parents take this same view, and practically prevent their children from entering heartily into religious work because of their deference to a false intellectual standard imposed by the public schools. "Wait till they get through school" is often the cry. "They can join the young people's society; they can serve on some committee; they can do some church work, then." A terrible procrastination is this—wait till they get through school and the religious sensibility is blunted; the head has outgrown the heart; the desire actively to serve God is dead, and a more fatal obstacle than parental indifference has supervened—the disinclination of the young person himself, which is likely to be strengthened by the cares and complexities of later life!

I am not looking at this matter from the standpoint alone of the religious teacher who desires more time and opportunity and leisure for his specialty, for this is the ground of the scientific psychologist as well.

"There is ground," says Professor Coe, "for a suspicion that the conditions under which a vast majority of adolescents are placed in our modern light and life tend to produce a state of habitual fatigue. Among these grounds may be named the tendency to overload the common-school and high-school curriculum, the amount of social life involving late hours, excitement, and unwholesome eating and drinking permitted to young adolescents and even expected of them, the multiplicity of interests that crowd out simplicity and repose, and finally the almost feverish intensity with which American youth enter into their too varied occupations. It would scarcely be an exaggeration to assert that sixteen-year-old girls and eighteen-year-old boys are expected to live two lives in one, the life of students and the life of men and women of the world." *

All this begets indifference or morbidness, and Professor Coe enumerates the following evils as likely to come in the train of this intellectual and social dissipation: worry, despondency, bad temper, over-sensitiveness, lack of decision in small matters, increased susceptibility to temptations of appetite and of sex.

But serious as these difficulties are in the way of Christian Nurture, they are not insuperable, or if they present a barrier too high to be overcome in the case of certain individuals, there are others whom every pastor can reach and help, and these will be his joy and pride. Besides, the very obstacles in our way should spur us on to devise means of overcoming them. No wise method of Christian Nurture should be carelessly passed by. No

* Coe, "The Spiritual Life."

plan which God has particularly blessed should be disdained. No effort should be too great which may overcome obstacles and accomplish the saving and training of the young, which will mean the saving of the Church of God from stagnation and decay.

On a wall of the Institution for the Blind in South Boston hangs the favorite motto of Samuel G. Howe, the great pioneer patron of the blind, "Obstacles are Things to be Overcome." The objects which the Christian minister has in view in training his young people for Christ and the church are surely vast enough, the rewards of success, even partial success, are surely inspiring enough to lead him to throw himself with whole-hearted enthusiasm against any difficulties, exclaiming, not only in the words of Samuel G. Howe, "*Obstacles are things to be overcome,*" but also: "Through Christ I can overcome obstacles. In His strength I can overcome the indifference of worldly parents. In His strength I can combat the material and coldly intellectual tendencies of the day. In His strength I can kindle and keep alive in many a young heart a spark of love for divine things which will some day, perhaps, be fanned into a mighty flame of devotion."

The fruitfulness of this work for the young is beyond all comparison. If as much effort, prayer, and agony were spent upon winning the children and youth as upon winning and edifying the adults, how incomparable would be the results? Think the matter over for a moment! What proportion of the average minister's time and thought is given to the adults of his congregation and how much to the children? Reckon up the hours spent on the two classes. Two services a Sunday, fifty two Sundays in the year, largely for grown people—an occasional five-minute sermon for the children, a Children's Sunday once a year, and the minister's sermonic duty to them is done.

But the adults! the sermon-steeped saints who little need them, or the sermon-hardened sinners who will not hear them, or from whose well-fortified consciences the truth will rebound like the cannon balls from the steel skin of a monitor—there must be something like a hundred homilies every year prepared for the edification of one class or the unsympathetic criticism of the other!

The midweek prayer-meeting is for the adult. To be sure the young people are welcomed, and are often berated if they do not attend, but the meeting has the mature Christian in view, and, if the young do participate, it often seems like an intrusion into the special preserves of their elders to which only the boldest are equal.

The Sabbath-school is largely for the young, but many ministers consider it very small concern of theirs. The superintendent and the teachers are responsible, and, as for the young people's meeting, some ministers—not many, I am glad to believe—resent it as an intrusion upon their valuable time if they are ever expected to attend.

Here are ten hours of prayer and planning and anxious thought given to the adults by many clergymen to one given to the young people, when the results of working for the young people compared with the results obtained in working for the adults are as ten to one. In other words, ten times the effort is, as a rule, spent on those who are ten times over the least susceptible.

I do not ask that this schedule be reversed and that ten hours be given to the young and one hour to the rest of the congregation, tho that division would be more reasonable than the proportion now often observed. But is it unreasonable to ask that the time and thought be equally divided? There are quite as many children and youth in our congregations, or there ought to be, as there are adults. There are more of them in our homes. If a line were drawn at the age of twenty-five in all Protestant parishes in America, more souls would be found below than above that line.

Is it unreasonable to ask, then, that the majority, whose needs are as great and whose openness to religious impression is much greater, should receive at least as much of the minister's time and thought as the less hopeful minority? We need to get over the impression so widely prevalent that the soul of a grown person is a little more valuable than the soul of a child, and that it is a greater triumph to win such a soul for the Kingdom. How often have I seen in our religious papers a statement like this: "There has been a revival of religion in

3

the parish of So-and-So, in which fifteen of the twenty converts were heads of families." Brother So-and-So often words his announcement of an awakening in such a way that one would think he was almost ashamed of the converts unless they had the distinction of being "heads of families." The note of triumph, it seems to me, belongs, if it belongs anywhere, in another announcement—not, "Twenty converts, most of them heads of families," but "Twenty converts, all of them children or youth; all of them to be heads of families; all of them consecrating the freshness and vigor of their best years to Christ; all of them giving, not the fag-end of worn-out lives to Christ, but the strength and beauty of their youth, as well as the maturity of their manhood and womanhood and the ripe mellowness of their old age."

Consider the life-insurance system of averages. A boy of fifteen may expect to have forty-five years yet to live; the man of fifty may expect less than twenty years of life. Suppose twenty boys and girls of fifteen are led in a time of awakening to decide honestly to live the Christian life. The aggregate expectation of these lives is nine hundred years—nine hundred years of service and influence, nine hundred years of prayer and praise, nine hundred years of pure living and noble striving. Almost a Methuselah's lifetime of work and worship! Twenty boyhoods and twenty youths and twenty manhoods and twenty old men all for Christ and His cause are won when the twenty boys are won. But when the twenty men in middle life, the much-heralded "heads of families" are counted, their aggregate expectation of life will be at the most about four hundred years. They will have much less than one-half the time of the boys to live. Their boyhood, youth, and young manhood are behind them. These years can not be used for Christ, and the sere and yellow leaf is not so valuable a gift as the bud and blossom, the flower and the fruit.

Besides, the possibilities of the youthful company are vastly greater. Of the man in middle life we say "What is he?" Of the old man, "What was he?" Of the youth: "What will he be?" And in that question of the future tense are possibilities that set the pulses bounding.

Polycarp was converted at nine years of age, we are told; Matthew Henry at eleven; Dr. Isaac Watts at nine, Bishop Hall when eleven, and Robert Hall when twelve. What parent would take the responsibility of keeping out of the visible Kingdom of God a possible Matthew Henry or a Robert Hall? What minister would not labor years to bring such a saint into the service of our Lord and feel that he was well repaid for his efforts? The boy in our family, in our Sunday-school, in our Christian Endeavor Society, may be the compeer of any one of these saints. At least he has a soul which in God's sight is precious enough to demand the supreme sacrifice. It is worth our while, our pains, and time to second Christ's effort to win the children and the youth whom He suffered to come unto Him.

A few years ago I stood in a most fascinating spot, the diamond-fields of Kimberley, South Africa. The diamondiferous blue earth had been taken out of the mines in great quantities and spread upon the "floors," so-called—fields of many acres in extent—where it should disintegrate in the air and sunshine so that the diamonds might be more easily extracted. For several months this blue earth lies on the fields carefully guarded before it is crushed and pulverized and the diamonds taken out. The fascination of the spot lies in the fact that every clod of clay which you may kick with your foot as you walk across the fields may contain a Kohinoor. To be sure, not every clod does contain a diamond, not one in a hundred of the lumps of earth contains a gem, but any lump may be rich in diamonds.

If it were certain that a brilliant lurked in every piece of earth, a walk across the diamond floors of Kimberley would indeed be a thrilling experience at least for the avaricious man. The children and youth with whom we have to deal contain within their natures a gem of great price. It is not a possibility; it is a certainty. The gem may be dimmed and dulled and lost. It may be saved and set in a king's diadem. The very possibility of winning such treasures may well cause the pastor's heart to glow as he thinks of the young people among whom God has called him to work.

Let us establish in our minds once for all these propositions:

First, very young people are capable of receiving and exercising divine grace.

Second, they are far, far more accessible to this grace than they will be in after-life. If this is true it would seem that the pastor's supreme duty to care for the young need no longer be argued.

The concurrent testimony of those who have been able to judge, those who have had large experience in soul-winning, will surely be of weight. Says Dr. Theodore L. Cuyler:

"It is no uncommon thing for children of seven or eight years of age to have received more mental cultivation than we formerly looked for at twelve or thirteen. What is now common was once thought a prodigy in the development of mind. . . . I will only remark that I have known a child at nine years of age better acquainted with the doctrines of religion than two-thirds of our church-members, and that I have been well acquainted with at least one case of conversion between five and six years of age."

Said Rev. Charles H. Spurgeon:

"I have, during the last year, received forty or fifty children into church-membership. Among those I have had at any time to exclude from the church, out of a church of twenty-seven hundred members, I have never had to exclude a single one who was received whilst yet a child. Teachers and superintendents should not merely believe in the *possibility* of early conversion, but in the *frequency* of it."

Said Dr. Stephen H. Tyng:

"I solemnly believe in the conversion of children. I can not say how young they may be brought to make an open profession of their faith and love for Christ, but I have seen as manifest evidences of the new-birth in children of six and eight years of age as I have ever seen in an adult. Shall I turn back those whom God Himself hath brought? Shall I refuse those whom God Himself has accepted?"

A few years ago on two separate occasions I made a canvass of some of the best-known Christian men of the country, ministers and laymen, in order to determine how many of them dated their religious experience to their early years, and also to find their opinion in regard to the expediency of church-membership for the young. The questions asked were:

First: At what age did you become a Christian?

Second: At what age did you make a public confession of Christ?

Third: Does your personal opinion incline you to the belief that it is well for children about the age of twelve years to make a public confession of Christ by uniting with His church?

Of course it was understood that such children gave such evidence as a child might be expected to give of

The Church of the Future

being Christ's disciple. Let me quote a few of these replies, for they are most illumining:

Rev. Charles F. Deems, D.D., LL.D., for so many years the popular and beloved pastor of the Church of the Strangers, New York, wrote:

"In reply to your inquiries, which I think very important, it gives me great pleasure to say that if to become a Christian means giving one's heart to Christ, I think I can say that with me that occurred at thirteen years of age. I was not fourteen years of age when I confessed Christ and publicly became a member of the Christian Church. Over this fact I have frequently heartfelt and sometimes enthusiastic rejoicing. It now seems to me so plain that if I had postponed that surrender a year longer I might never have become a Christian, for just after this my father's home was broken up and I went off to college.

"My personal experience leads me to believe that it is well for children to make a public confession of Christ by uniting with some church *just as early as they feel like it*. I mean by that, that if a child is old enough to love the Lord Jesus Christ as his divine Savior, and to express a wish to do something to show that love, he is old enough to become a member of any church. The wretched folly of church discipline of past ages has been to assume that an intellectual comprehension of some creed was necessary for church-membership. A real Christian church is a body of people who love the Lord Jesus Christ with a love that passeth knowledge.

"Moreover, I have made this observation after a ministry of over fifty years. A larger proportion of children who have made a confession of Christ by joining a church before they were fifteen years old have held out faithfully than of all those who have become church-members after they were twenty-five. I am very sure that no earnest child, however young, who applied for membership in the Church of the Strangers would be refused on the ground of his age."

Rev. Abbott E. Kittredge, D.D., Pastor of the Madison Avenue Reformed Church, New York:

"1. It was, I think, when I was eight years old that I gave my heart to the Savior.

"2. I joined the church when I was seventeen years old. It was not considered wise in those days for children to unite with the church, but I believe in my case it was a great mistake. I should have been greatly helped and comforted had I been as a child a church-member.

"3. Your third question has already been partly answered. I most certainly think it wise for children who give evidence of faith in Christ and a new heart to unite with the visible church. In fact, I believe it is our duty to receive them, for the Shepherd can surely keep the lambs if He can keep the sheep."

Rev. John Hall, D.D., LL.D., the late lamented pastor of the Fifth Avenue Presbyterian Church, New York:

"In reply to your inquiries I have to say, with profound gratitude to God, that I was brought up in the closest connection with the church, learned the 'Shorter Catechism' in my home, attended Sabbath-school, and,

I think, believed in the Savior for years before becoming a communicant. This step I was permitted to take at the age of fourteen, after passing through the communicants' class of a faithful pastor.

"I think where children of intelligence desire to be members, they should be received. At the age of twelve or thirteen years there is the capacity to understand the truth. I receive such, *where they are in Christian homes.* I would not encourage the step in those who are not in such homes, at this early age, for this reason: that in unfavorable surroundings some such relapse into carelessness, and are then less disposed to come under spiritual influence. 'Oh, yes, joined the church. I know what that is; I went through all that.' To avoid the risk of such results, in certain cases I favor a time of learning and 'probation' before profession on the part of those not blessed with a godly home."

Rev. William F. Warren, D.D., President of Boston University:

"To your first question I know not what answer to give. Blessed with Christian parents, I was so dedicated to God in prayer and Christian nurture from the very beginning that I know not what germs of divine life were unfolding within me from the first. I can not remember when I began to pray and to take a certain pleasure in acts of devotion. Taught, however, that I was not a Christian, it seemed to me when I was about fifteen years of age an inconsistent thing for me to continue to pray. Accordingly, I abandoned the practise, and made trial of the barren life of the prodigal son. Three years later, I returned with godly sorrow to my

Father's house, whence I hope to go out no more forever. With wiser pastoral care I doubt whether I should ever have gone out at all.

"I joined the church in my eighteenth year.

"My personal experience leads me to believe that all Christian children should be treated as such, and that from the beginning they should be taught that they are probationary members of the church, to be received into full membership with public recognition and responsibilities so soon as thoroughly instructed and tested in the Christian life."

Rev. A. J. Gordon, D.D., then pastor of the Clarendon-Street Baptist Church, Boston:

"1. I was converted at sixteen.

"2. I was baptized and joined the church at sixteen.

"3. Later experience has taught me the advisability of bringing into the church children of twelve years or younger who give proof of conversion."

James B. Angell, LL.D., President of the University of Michigan, Ann Arbor, Mich.:

"1. At the age of seventeen years, when a sophomore in college.

"2. At the age of twenty I joined the church, tho my profession of faith was public from the first.

"3. Decidedly yes, if the child has come to a fixed purpose to lead a Christian life, without forcing or under pressure, and is likely to be under the guidance of discreet parents or friends. But if the child has formed the purpose under some strong pressure of excitement and can not rely on the help of wise parents or friends, caution should be used. In other words, one needs to distinguish between a passing gust of emotion and a natural, thoughtful purpose such as a child of twelve is often capable of cherishing under favoring circumstances."

Rev. S. J. McPherson, D.D., pastor of the Second Presbyterian Church, Chicago, Ill. :

"1. I became a Christian and I joined the church at the age of fourteen years.

"My personal experience has convinced me that the earlier Christians unite with the church the better it is for them and for that training-school of Christ, the church. They have less to unlearn, they are less hampered by consolidated habits, they grow more naturally into Christian character, they save the years from waste, and their special gifts are far more likely to open properly. I regard it as a great misfortune for any man to come into the church late rather than early. I have rarely known a child who became a Christian and a church-member at the age of twelve, who was trained in a wise and devoted Christian household, to 'fall away' from his covenant. There is much to be said on the matter, and it is, to my mind, wholly on one side."

Hon. Franklin Fairbanks, St. Johnsbury, Vt. :

"1. I can not tell when I became a Christian. I think I always was, for I can not remember when I did not love my Savior. This I owe to faithful, godly parents.

"2. I united with the church when I was fourteen years old.

"3. Yes, I do believe that it is well for children, if

Christians, to make a public confession at twelve years of age. For thirty years I have been superintendent of our Sunday-school, and I have carefully watched Christian children who at an early age publicly confessed Christ. I give it as my observation that the percentage of those who hold on, live exemplary lives, and grow strong in Christian character is *very much* greater with children than with those who make confession of faith in later years."

Rev. Washington Gladden, D.D., pastor of the First Congregational Church, Columbus, O. :

"1. I can not answer.

"2. I became a member of the church at the age of seventeen.

"3. Children trained in Christian families ought, in my judgment, to come into the church at the age of twelve years, in some cases earlier. I have received a large number who were under twelve. There are risks attending this early membership, but the risks of permitting children to grow away from the church are far greater."

Rev. J. L. Withrow, D.D., pastor of the Park Street Church, Boston:

"1 and 2. I united with the church under thirteen years of age. I think I had accepted Christ as my Savior years before.

"3. My experience does lead me to encourage such. Of course, if children have no home care, nor special church oversight and encouragement, they are more likely to fall away than if they were more mature in

44

judgment and experience. But taking everything together, I would rather trust them at the beginning at that age than when older."

Samuel B. Capen, President American Board Commissioners Foreign Missions, Boston:

"1. I do not know certainly. There was a period of about two years in my life, when I was between sixteen and eighteen years of age, in which I think I would have taken a decided position as a Christian if it had been the custom of that day, as it is now, for the church to look carefully after the boys and expect them to be committed.

"2. I was eighteen years of age when I united with the church.

"3. Yes, most emphatically. I believe those who unite with the church when young and come thereby under some responsibility average better than those who come later in life. One of my children joined our church when nine years of age, and the other at ten. In our late war many men were deserters and proved cowards in various ways, but there is no case on record of a 'drummer-boy' who ever ran away."

President C. F. Thwing, of Adelbert College, once addressed a letter similar to the one I have referred to a picked company of conspicuously useful, Christian men; they happened to be the corporate members of the American Board of Commissioners of Foreign Missions. Of the one hundred and forty-nine who replied, every one of whom was a tower of strength in later life in some church of Christ, nine-tenths believed that they experienced conversion before they were twenty, while only fourteen were over twenty. All but thirty had joined the church before they were twenty. Twenty-nine declared that they became Christians when "very young," or so young that they did not remember when they were not Christians. Twenty-one others were younger than twelve when they intelligently made the great decision, and one hundred and five of the one hundred and forty-nine made it before they were eighteen years of age.

These facts surely are significant; they would be startling were they not in a general way so familiar. But so is the law of gravitation familiar. Nevertheless it must be reckoned with by every intelligent being. The law of children in the Kingdom is declared not only by Scriptures, but by experience. It was never put so well as our Lord put it: "Suffer little children to come unto me and forbid them not, for *of such* is the kingdom of heaven."

I once made somewhat similar inquiries of the Christian business men of Portland, Me., where I was then a pastor. This inquiry, to be sure, related to early churchgoing, but it bears strongly upon the particular point we are considering, for this early churchgoing resulted in the early formation of Christian character. My questions were as follows:

"DEAR SIR:—Desiring to learn if the present decline in church attendance, so often complained of, is a re-

action from Puritanical strictness in the past, as is frequently alleged, or is due to laxity of parental authority,
will you be so kind as to tell me—

"1. Whether in early life you were required to attend
church regularly?

"2. If so, did such compulsion render churchgoing
irksome or repulsive to you?

"Any other facts from personal experience, or from
that of others bearing upon this point, will be gratefully
received."

Of the fifty persons to whom I sent these questions,
forty-five replied. They represented different denominations and embraced a large proportion of the prominent men in the churches. Of these forty-five, three
were not required to go to church when young, and
forty-two were. Of these three who were not required
to go, two went of their own accord. Two others of my
correspondents make a distinction between being required to go and being solemnly and earnestly urged to
go; that is, between physical and moral compulsion.
But that kind of compulsion came within the intent of
my inquiry. Where it is the regularly expected thing
for children to attend church, as much as to attend
school, that is the best kind of compulsion.

Of those forty-five, then, from whom I have received
answers, forty-two were required to go to church as children; two were not required to go, but nevertheless
went.

Forty-two did not consider churchgoing irksome or

repulsive; one did consider it irksome, but not repulsive; one considered it irksome, but not because of the compulsion; and one did not go, and so of course did not find church attendance repulsive.

So you see the testimony of these forty-five representative Christian men, obtained without collusion or knowledge as to the use to which their testimony would be put, almost with unanimity tells that their early training required church attendance, and that such attendance did not drive them away from church even for a time.

In view of these facts, what becomes of the threadbare and sickly plea, "I am afraid to require any religious duties of my child lest he acquire a distaste for them?" Just exactly as sensible is the plea, "I am afraid to require any ablutions of my child lest he acquire a distaste for a clean face."

Now, what do these statistics show us in regard to the probable effect of churchgoing upon the boys and girls of to-day?

So far as this testimony goes, we learn that the chances of the boys and girls of the present generation becoming eminent and useful Christians are as forty-four to one in favor of those who attend church, as forty-two to three in favor of those who are required to attend; and the chances that they will be repelled and disgusted by such requirement are only as one to forty-five.

Or, to put the matter in still another way, so far as

48

these testimonies prove anything, they prove that, of those who become particularly eminent and useful in the church in mature life, nearly ninety-eight per cent. went to church regularly as boys, ninety-four per cent. were required to go, and ninety-six per cent were not repelled from church, even for a little while, by such requirement.

In his fascinating book, "The Psychology of Religion," from which I have before quoted, Dr. E. D. Starbuck, after exhaustive inquiries and elaborate distinctions, comes to these conclusions:

"Conversion does not occur with the same frequency at all periods in life. It belongs *almost exclusively* to the years between ten and twenty-five. *The number of instances outside that range appear few and scattered. That is, conversion is a distinctively adolescent phenomenon.* It is a singular fact also that within this period the conversions do not distribute themselves equally among the years. In the rough we may say they begin to occur at seven or eight years, and increase in numbers gradually to ten or eleven, and then rapidly to sixteen; rapidly decline to twenty, and gradually fall away after that and become rare after thirty. One may say that if conversion has not occurred before twenty the chances are small that it will ever be experienced."

The opinions and research of the psychologist and the philosopher confirm the experience of the practical men of affairs. The psychologist's words sound almost like a knell: "One may say that if conversion has not occurred before twenty, the chances are small that it will ever be experienced."*

What, then, is the conclusion of this whole matter? Is it not that the Lord's reiterated command, "Feed my lambs, feed my little sheep," comes to us with redoubled power? Here among the children and youth is the choicest garden spot in all the Lord's domain. Why spend all the time in reclaiming the desert when the soil of youth will yield thirty-fold, sixty-fold, a hundred-fold? Is there any excuse which can avail for not entering this field? Is it sufficient for the pastor to say: "I am too busy, too preoccupied; I can not bother myself with the children"? Is study more important? Is the Greek Testament as imperative as the spotless page of the child's soul? Is the morning sermon the matter of supremest importance? Is the midweek prayer-meeting of the church to be elaborately prepared for and never missed, while the young people's meeting has the go-by? Shall we spend all our time digging in the scoriæ of the burnt-out emotions of the aged or the middle-aged, and forget the virgin gold-mine of youthful love and enthusiasm which will so richly reward our toil?

Is it sufficient for the pastor to say, "I am not adapted to work among children and youths"? Said to me one minister of noble proportions—noble physical proportions—"I am *too* big to go to the young people's meeting

* Starbuck, "The Psychology of Religion."

50

The Church of the Future

—the little fish don't like to have a whale swim into their school!"

Perhaps it would have been appropriate to quote to this brother some familiar words about becoming as a little child before one enters the kingdom of heaven. But let us come back once more to the question with which our lecture began: What is the ministry for? What is all preparatory study for? What is the ultimate object of the weary delving over Greek and Hebrew construction? What is the object of the morning sermon and the pastoral call and the midweek meeting but to establish and build up Christian character?

If this can best be done in large part in labor for the young, then labor for the young becomes one of the chief concerns of the true minister, and all other interests, important as they are, will give this labor its rightful and exalted place. The minister who is too busy or too preoccupied to care for the young, is too busy to build up his church. The true servant of God will find the time and make the opportunity. He will adapt himself to this work, however few were his gifts in this direction originally. He will gain for himself the young heart that he may win the young; so that at the last, when his account is demanded, he may say, "Here am I, Lord, and the children whom thou hast given me."

METHODS OF CHRISTIAN NURTURE
PAST AND PRESENT

Chapter II

METHODS OF CHRISTIAN NURTURE PAST AND PRESENT

JEWISH METHODS OF RELIGIOUS NURTURE—CHILD LIFE IN THE BIBLE — THE VARIETY AND MINUTENESS OF THE NAME FOR "CHILD"—JEWISH TRAINING EMINENTLY RELIGIOUS—CHILD LIFE IN THE BIBLE A CONSTANT GROWTH—LATER METHODS OF CHRISTIAN NURTURE—THE HOME PREEMINENT—THE FAMILY NOT THE ONLY FORCE THAT MOLDS CHARACTER — GREAT MEN FROM CHRISTIAN HOMES — THE JUKES FAMILY AND THE EDWARDS FAMILY—THE CHRISTLESS HOME—THE SUNDAY-SCHOOL A CHIEF METHOD OF CHRISTIAN NURTURE—UNDESERVED CRITICISM OF THE SUNDAY-SCHOOL—FOCUSING THE TRUTH UPON THE HEART — THE SUNDAY-SCHOOL AS A HARVEST FIELD — THE SUNDAY-SCHOOL PRAYER - MEETING—THE PASTOR'S CLASS—THE JUNIOR ENDEAVOR SOCIETY—THE USE OF THE CATECHISM—HOW IT CAN BE USED IN JUNIOR ENDEAVOR WORK—STUDYING THE CHURCH COVENANT AND CREED—THE YOUNG MEN'S CHRISTIAN ASSOCIATION—BOYS' BRIGADES AND BOYS' CLUBS—MISSION CIRCLES, KING'S DAUGHTERS, AND KING'S SONS—BANDS OF MERCY AND TEMPERANCE LEGIONS.

THE training of the church of the future has always been a matter of concern to the church of the present. We thank God for this. Otherwise there would be no church of the present. Some generations have been much more solicitous than others respecting this training, and have used wiser means and used them more persistently, and of course these generations have reaped the

55

largest results in numbers and in the character of converts added to the church.

No people has been more solicitous on this point of religious nurture and training than the Jews of old, and the early Christian era seems to have taken up in full the interest of the Jews in the training of the youth. The Bible, when read in the light of Jewish history and customs, becomes a treatise on child nurture which we do well to study. I may perhaps be allowed to quote a few pages from studies I have already published concerning child life in the Bible, based in part on Dr. Ginsburg's writings on this subject.

"The Scriptures leave no doubt in the minds of most readers in regard to the supreme importance they attach to the early and careful religious training of the young. The Bible treats child life as it does every other subject, in accordance with the customs in vogue at the time it was written; and from its general tenor we have every reason to suppose that it approves and supports these existing customs. Thus, in order fitly to appreciate the child life of the Bible, we must inquire how children were regarded, what was their education, and how much attention was paid to them by the Jews. When we turn to this subject we are surprised to find how large is its literature. The very number and variety and minuteness of the names for ' child ' show the importance of child life and the close scrutiny with which it was watched. There were no less than nine of these names, denoting the different stages of the child's history. Besides the general names for son or daughter, there was

one that meant 'the newly born' child; another that
meant 'the suckling'; another still that referred to the
time just before weaning; and a fourth that meant the
weaned child. When he becomes a little older and begins to go alone with short and tottering steps, he is
called *taph*, or 'the quickly stepping one,'—'the little
trotter,' as we might phrase it. When he becomes still
older, and is able to help his parents, he is called *elem*,
or 'the strong.' When able to defend and take care of
himself, he is *naar*, or 'free'; and when he has attained
his majority and is fit for military service, then he is
bachur, or 'matured,'—'the ripe one.' What a watch-
ful eye do all these names indicate! By following them
along we can almost see the development and growth of
the Jewish youth and maiden. Immediately after the
birth of the child, it was washed, rubbed with salt, and
wrapped in swaddling-clothes, and the announcement of
its birth was hailed with joy, especially if it was a son.
When the boy was eight days old, he received his name,
and the rite of circumcision was performed. Twenty-
two days after this, his father redeemed him by giving
to the priest thirty shekels of the sanctuary, thus ac-
knowledging in a most forcible way that he belonged to
the Lord who gave him.

"The education of the Jewish children, as we have
seen, was eminently a religious training. ' If you ask a
Jew,' says Josephus, ' concerning any matter concerning
the law, he can more easily explain it than tell his own
name; since we learn it from the first beginning of intelligence, it is, as it were, graven on our souls.' ' The
Jews,' says Philo, ' look on their laws as revelations
from God, and are taught them from their earliest in-

fancy; they bear the image of the law on their souls.'
The children were bound to worship God in His sanctuary 'as soon as they were able,' was the regulation,
'with the help of their fathers' hand, to climb the flight
of steps into the temple courts.' This was the way Samuel was trained, and David and John and Timothy; and
because of this training they became Samuel and David
and John and Timothy. It depends upon the parents
and teachers of to-day what the next generations shall
be, and it depends upon what they do and teach to-day.
We have the clean, white, smooth tablets in our hands,
in the souls of our children; what shall we write there-
on, religion or worldliness?

"Again, child life in the Bible is always represented
as a constant growth. Over and over again we are told
the child Samuel grew before the Lord. 'And Samuel
grew, and the Lord was with him.' Of John the Baptist as a child it is said, 'He grew and waxed strong
in spirit.' And even of our Lord Himself the same
words are used. We should shrink from using such an
expression if we had no inspired authority for it. The
Savior grew, increased in spiritual power! 'Why,' we
should say, 'it is almost blasphemy to speak thus.' But
the Bible says so. 'And the child grew and waxed
strong in spirit, and the grace of God was on him.'
This idea is universal throughout the Bible. To become
religious does not make a prodigy of a boy or a girl. It
does not ripen and mature the character all at once. It
is not a hot-bed process. The religious child is still a
child, needing training, instruction, warning, and we
must not expect or look for anything else. When we
see the seed sown in fickle April weather springing up

in April and flowering in April and bearing fruit in
April, when we see saplings grow visibly before our
eyes, expand in girth and throw out far-reaching roots
and gigantic limbs in a single season, then may we expect to see a child Christian become an old Christian in
a week; but till then we need not expect to see any such
phenomena. Of course a child's ideas of religion are
crude, of course his knowledge of duty is imperfect, of
course he falls into childish blunders and errors; there
would be no such thing as growth in grace were it otherwise. But the acorn contains the oak, the straight,
branchless sapling is the forerunner of the wide-spread-
ing shade-tree; in the child Christian's heart lie the
germs of the aged Christian's experience.

"I think there is a lesson of vast importance in these
considerations of child life in the Bible. I beg for it
careful and prayerful attention, for it is a lesson which
the church has often neglected to its own sad hurt. It
is this: It is natural, it is possible, it is desirable, for
children to grow up into Christian manhood and womanhood without experiencing any sharp and sudden trans-
ition from an evil life to a good life. Nay, it is not only
possible and desirable, it is the thing we ought to expect; it ought to be as common for young children to be
born into the kingdom of God as to be born into the
world. It is possible and natural for children to be converted at their mother's knee, and never know the time
when they did not love the Savior. And this should not
be something rare, occasional, remarkable; a phenomenon, a thing to excite remark, like a comet or a meteor.
It should be the usual, expected thing that children of
religious parents should choose to live for the Savior as

early as they are able to make any choice, and should be received into the church and receive its nurturing, fostering care.

"Search the child biographies of the Bible through and see if this idea is not borne out. Was Samuel a wise, independent man before he heard God speak his name? Was John the Baptist allowed to sow any wild oats before he became a preacher of righteousness? Could Timothy better have strengthened the early church if he had been a *roué* in his youth? Did Jesus Himself pass through no period of boyhood growth? Did even He not require thirty long years of training before He called a single disciple to Him?

"The doctrines of conversion, conviction of sin, and regeneration have been monstrously perverted when they have been made to teach that in every case, whatever the natural disposition or early training, there must be a sudden, conscious, awful wrench from old ways of living; for such a view shuts out all childish conversions, and makes a youth of sin indispensable to an old age of godliness. This explains many of the terrible revelations which praying parents have had concerning their sons and daughters. They have looked and longed and prayed for a sudden, thrilling conversion and experience for their children, rather than for a very early, quiet turning to God and growth in grace. This sudden, thrilling experience never came, but ruin and disgrace and heartache have come, because the parents have not practically believed in a religious childhood. We believe that the Bible teaches that it is not necessary for young, innocent children to agonize over their sins, and mourn and weep like gray-haired offenders, and then come out of a terrible darkness into a marvelous light. We need not look for any such experience. The dawn comes gradually, the lightning with a blinding flash; but the daylight is far more useful than the lightning's glare. It depends very largely upon Christian parents and pastors whether the day-dawn from on high shall come into children's lives while they are very young and illuminate all their eternity. Let us plan for this, pray for this, expect this, and to the children will belong the blessed experience of never knowing a time when they were not Christians." *

We must pass from the child life of the Bible to later times. The methods of Christian nurture employed in the Catholic Church and in the early reformation era we may pass over without comment, as these lectures do not profess to give a history of the Christian training of youth, but to deal largely with some modern methods applicable to-day.

In the post-Reformation period the catechism and the confirmation class played a large part in the training of children and youth for the service of the King. For the most part these instrumentalities did their work admirably and were well fitted for that day and generation, as indeed they are for many churches at the present day. It was a sad day for many a church when it gave up catechetical instruction.

Let us come to certain methods of Christian nurture which are common at the present time. Foremost and

* Clark, " Children and the Church."

61

preeminent among these is and always will be, the instruction in the home. Nothing can ever take the place of home training. At the best other methods can only supplement and round out the nurture of the home, or can make up in some little measure for the defects or lack of home training. The mother's knee, the father's kindly care, form the very best possible means for the Christian nurture of children. And yet we find that, even in Christian homes, children sometimes grow up wild and reckless or hard and inapproachable to gospel truth. Why is this so? Bushnell gives one reason in a characteristic sentence:

"Because," he answers, "many persons, remarkable for their piety, are yet very disagreeable persons, and that, too, by reason of some very marked defect in their religious character. They display just that spirit and act in just that manner which is likely to make religion odious—the more odious the more urgently they commend it. Sometimes they appear well to the world one remove distant from them, they shine well in their written biography, but one living in their family will know what others do not, and, if their children turn out badly, will never be at a loss for the reason."*

But the defects of cross-grained parents whose theology is better than their practise are not the only cause of the aberrations of the children of such homes. The family, after all, is in our complicated life but one of the forces

* Bushnell, "Christian Nurture."

that are at work in molding the character of every boy and girl. The influence of nineteen hours in the best home on earth can be counteracted by five hours at school. The carefully nurtured boy, who for a dozen years has been kept from contamination in the home, may have a foul seed planted in his heart by a half-hour's contact with the rotten life of an unclean boy to whom he looks up as his elder and superior. The careful training of years may be undone, in a measure at least, by an evil book or picture, or by a persistent sneer at religious things. So there is need of buttressing the best home on earth with other influences which shall help to mold the character for God.

Before passing on to speak of these adjuncts of the home in Christian training, I would like to take a moment to deny the impression prevalent in many quarters that an unusual proportion of rakes and ne'er-do-wells come out of Christian homes. If the statistics were at hand, it would surprise every one to see what a vast proportion of the world's best and most forceful men and women have come out of Christian homes. I believe that it would be no exaggeration to say, from the partial and incomplete investigations that I have made, that, while the proportion of avowedly Christian homes to non-Christian is only about one to four, of the men who have made their mark in the world, who have won true success in the all-round field of human achievement, three-fourths of them have come out of Christian homes.

One-fourth of the homes have produced three-fourths of the world's best men and women.

Of course these figures can not be absolutely verified. I shall not quarrel with any one who disputes them, but when we go through any modern dictionary of biography, so far as we can judge of the Christian character of the parents, we find that the praying mothers of distinguished sons have been vastly in the majority.

The statement has been going the rounds of the papers of late, that fifty per cent of the eminent people embraced in a certain famous biographical dictionary were the sons or daughters of clergymen. This is probably an exaggeration, but, if it is even approximately true, what becomes of the old saw about "ministers' sons and deacons' daughters"? It was Dean Swift, I believe, who, in view of the acknowledged preeminence of clergymen's children, advocated an endowment of the British parsonage for the propagation of a superior race which should bless the world, because bred from choicest stock.

A study and comparison have recently been made by Dr. A. E. Winship, of the descendants of the famous criminal vagabond, Jukes, and the descendants of Jonathan Edwards. The results are most astonishing, and doubtless if it were possible to make such studies and comparisons in other families, the influence of a godly home would always be seen even down to the third and fourth generation. Let me quote a few paragraphs from Mr. Winship's book:

Christian Nurture Past and Present

"The descendants of the Jukes family to the number of twelve hundred have been traced, while fourteen hundred members of the Edwards family have been studied and tabulated. The Jukes were notorious law-breakers, while the Edwards family has furnished practically no law-breakers and a great array of more than one hundred lawyers, thirty judges, and the most eminent law professor in the country. . . . None of the Jukes had the equivalent of a common-school education, while there are few of the Edwards family that have not had more than that. Few were satisfied with less than an academy or seminary, if they did not go to college. Yale alone has graduated more than one hundred and twenty of the family. . . . Of the Jukes four hundred and forty were more or less viciously diseased. The Edwards family were healthy and long-lived. The Jukes neglected all religious privileges, defied and antagonized the church and all that it stands for, while the Edwards family has more than a hundred clergymen, missionaries, and theological professors, many of the most eminent in the country's history. . . . Not one of the Jukes was ever elected to a public office, while more than eighty of the family of Jonathan Edwards have been especially honored. . . . The Jukes lacked the physical and moral courage as well as the patriotic purpose to enlist, but there were seventy-five officers in the army and navy in the family of Mr. Edwards. One spinster of the family residing in Detroit expressed much regret that she had no husband. The reason she gave was highly complimentary to the sterner sex, because she had no husband to send to the Civil War. . . . The Jukes were as far removed as possible from literature. They not only

never created any, but they never read anything that
could by any stretch of imagination be styled good reading. In the Edwards family some sixty have obtained
prominence in authorship or editorial life. Whatever
the Jukes stand for, the Edwards family does not; whatever weakness the Jukes represent, finds its antidote in
the Edwards family, which has cost the country nothing
in pauperism, in crime, in hospital or asylum service.
On the contrary it represents the highest usefulness in
invention, manufacture, commerce, founding of asylums
and hospitals, establishing and developing missions, pro-
jecting and energizing the best philanthropy."

But, alas! all homes are not Christian homes; not one-
half, scarcely one-fourth of all the households where
shines the evening lamp, are even nominally Christian,
and in many where the name of Christ is professed, and
He is nominally honored as the Head of the household,
there is but little of that direct, aggressive Christian influence which insures the early acceptance of Christ by
every child and constant development in the Christian
graces.

Some writers who exalt the home as the one sole and
sufficient means for Christian nurture, apparently leave
out of consideration the great multitude of Christless
homes. If we should admit that the home is sufficient
for one-fourth of the children who crowd our streets,
who come from the right sort of homes, what shall be
done for the other three-fourths? For them there is
no direct Christian influence in the home; they must

be trained for Christ elsewhere if they are trained at all.

Thus is impressed upon us from still another point of view the vast importance of wise, systematic Christian training.

The Sunday-school naturally presents itself as one of the chief and most important modern methods of Christian nurture. I have no sympathy with those who, as is the fashion in some quarters, depreciate this method or decry it altogether because it has not attained to perfection. It is true that in some Sunday-schools and in some classes in the best Sunday-schools a milk-and-water diet is given to the pupils. It is the Bible-and-water rather than the undiluted truth. Sacred geography and sacred history are often taught instead of the personal application of personal religion. The pattern of the ram's horns that the Israelites used in blowing down the walls of Jericho, and the particular kind of fish that swallowed Jonah, are often the staple subjects of discussion, while the teacher forgets to reason about temperance, righteousness, and judgment to come. But with all these defects—and a brilliant lecturer might use more than one hour in pointing out the mistakes of Sunday-schools as well as the mistakes of Moses—the incalculable value of the Sunday-school can not be overestimated, or the debt of gratitude diminished that the world owes to Robert Raikes.

Moreover, in this frequent denunciation and criticism

67

indulged in some quarters, the real, downright, conscientious work that multitudes of teachers put into the preparation and teaching of the lesson is often overlooked. Few know the hours and hours that are spent each week by tens of thousands of earnest Christians before they meet their Sunday-school classes. Few on earth hear the prayers or count the efforts of the majority of these devoted men and women, while the weakness or imbecility of the small minority is held up to ridicule.

The great fault of our Sunday-school teaching, if I may be allowed a single criticism, is that the truth is not often enough focused upon the hearts of the pupils. It is presented, but it is not driven home. Too much time is spent upon the generalities of the lesson, too little upon its application. Some Sunday-schools go on month after month and year after year, and there is no effort put forth to lead the scholar to make the great decision which we call conversion. In a great many schools this defect is remedied, and in all it may be remedied, by occasionally giving an evangelistic turn to the Sunday-school; by holding a few times each year a Sunday-school prayer-meeting immediately after the Sunday-school. Let me repeat the suggestions elsewhere made in regard to this meeting, which has proved such a harvest-time of ingathering in many Sunday-schools:

"Let the pastor or superintendent, or some judicious teacher, take charge of the meeting, and in a few direct, forcible words tell the children what it is to be a Christian; that Jesus longs to receive the smallest one; that it is a matter of choice for the child as well as for the man; and that Christianity is best shown by consistent, every-day living for Jesus at home, at school, and on the street.

"At the first meeting it may be well to ask all those children to rise who are willing to think the matter over seriously and to try to decide before next Sunday whether or not they will be Christians. It is my experience that a large number will rise at such an invitation; some out of sympathy with others, and many because they sincerely desire, in a childish way, to become the followers of Jesus. In the week that intervenes they will have time to think the matter over, and, if they have Christian parents, they should be urged to talk with their parents, then with their Sunday-school teachers, or some experienced friend.

"The next Sunday all these children, and very likely others, will remain to the Sunday-school prayer-meeting, and it may be well to ask them how many have thought the matter over carefully, and have finally decided to devote their lives to the Savior. It would seem best to make the decision appear a very plain and simple matter, but also a very serious matter, and to warn the boys and girls that they must make no pledges lightly or without full determination to carry them out. The great danger at this stage is that some, influenced by others, and with a feeble, half-formed determination to do better, will pledge themselves without really meaning anything by it; but this danger can largely be guarded against by a few words of serious explanation of the nature of the

Christian life, and of its being a matter of eternal import, and therefore not to be trifled with.

"The serious may further be sifted out from the frivolous by asking all the children who wish to know more about the Christian life, and who are really in earnest to be followers of the Savior, to come to the pastor's house some week-day, appointing one day for the girls and another for the boys. For the most part, only those who are really in earnest will accept such an invitation; and the opportunity this will give for private, personal talk with each of the children will be invaluable.

"After four or five such Sunday-school prayer-meetings, followed by such supplementary meetings at the pastor's house, it will be easy to sift the merely impulsive from the deeply serious or truly converted; and then it might be well to present to the boys and girls some simple pledge to which they shall sign their names, and which they can keep in their Bibles, and read over every day until it is ingrained into their minds. Every pastor will choose to make out his own pledge, perhaps, but I would suggest the following, as very simple and yet comprehensive:

"'Trusting in the Lord Jesus Christ for strength, I promise Him that I will strive to do whatever He would like to have me do; that I will pray to Him and read the Bible every day, and that, just so far as I know how, *throughout my whole life I will try to lead a Christian life.*

"'Signed, ——— ———.'

"The children, as we have said, should be encouraged in every way to talk with their parents and other friends about the matter, and perhaps, if they are quite young,

70

should take the pledge home and show it to their parents before they sign it. Very few parents will refuse to allow their children to sign such a pledge, and it will please them to know that everything that is done for their boys and girls is open and above-board. And now the real work of Christian nurture begins. The start has been made, the entering wedge has been driven, the door has been opened for the admission of the Spirit, and now comes the pastoral training and all the many good influences which an active church can throw around its children." *

The pastor's class is another and often a most invaluable means of training the young people in the distinctive things of the Christian life and in the duties and doctrines of the church. If you will pardon an allusion to a personal experience at this point, I have always found that the formation of a pastor's class for a few weeks early in the year following upon the Sunday-school prayer-meeting which I have just described, was an invaluable adjunct of these prayer-meetings. It gathered up the results. It gave me a personal acquaintance with the boys and girls. It gave me an opportunity to know something about their difficulties and their doubts. It enabled me to make plain the way of salvation and the path into the Kingdom. It insured every year an ingathering of young people into the church who knew what the church was, what it stood for, and what it demanded of them.

* Clark, "Children and the Church."

Training the Church of the Future

I hope it will not be considered boastful when I say that every year of my pastorate there were accessions, numbering usually from thirty to one hundred, most of them from the ranks of the young. I speak of this not because I had or have any peculiar gifts or used any unusual or startling methods to bring about these results. I was an average pastor in an average community, and what was done in those churches can in like measure be done in every church throughout the land. No evangelist was employed, tho I have no prejudice against wise evangelists, but rather rejoice exceedingly in their labors. But the methods adopted were those of the Sunday-school, the Sunday-school prayer-meeting, the pastor's class, and the young people's society, of which I shall speak in a later lecture.

I am not dealing with theories or fanciful suggestions, but with plans which might be marked, as the old lady marked the promises in her Bible, "T. and P."—Tried and Proved.

If young people are to be taken into the church at all, it is obviously most important that they should understand what they are doing and what the church believes; at least that they should know the great fundamental doctrines of the church which are level with the child's comprehension. What better place is there than the pastor's class to provide just such instruction and to prepare for intelligent church-membership?

It will not be necessary for the burdened pastor to

continue this class throughout the year, nor will it necessarily take a great amount of his time. A few weeks of training and instruction each year will fit the boys and girls who have made the choice of Christ for an intelligent confession of His name. The Junior Endeavor Society gives an admirable opportunity for just such instruction. There could not be a better pastor's class—the pastor taking fifteen or twenty minutes of the Junior hour for a few weeks or months, as he may see fit, for catechetical instruction.

The catechisms and manuals for such training are innumerable, ranging from the Westminster Shorter Catechism to the simplest and briefest modern statement of the essential truths of salvation.

This subject of catechetical instruction is of sufficient consequence to occupy the whole time devoted to a lecture. "No church ever grew strong, or, having grown strong, held its strength, without a catechism," is the dictum of an eminent divine. This may be an exaggeration, but the importance, if not of a catechism, at least of catechetical instruction, can scarcely be exaggerated. I have elsewhere suggested to Junior superintendents very urgently the catechetical methods. Perhaps I may be allowed to repeat here some things that I have already said:

"My suggestion is simply this, that we should use for ten minutes of each Junior hour manuals of question and answer in which the boys and girls may learn the doc-

73

trines of their own church, its history, and its work, and also lessons in clean, upright living, obedience, reverence, humility, and faithfulness.

"All these virtues, to be sure, are treated in every well-regulated junior society, sooner or later, through the prayer-meeting topics; but it seems to me that *through questions that can be asked and answers that can be learned* these greatest truths which Christ came to teach, and for which our churches stand, should be firmly planted in the little minds with which we have to deal.

"I do not know how this can be done in any other way so well as by some manual of instruction which used to be called 'the catechism,' and for which there is still no better name.

"I hope it will be fully understood, however, that I do not advocate giving all the time, or even most of it, to this instruction. The Junior Society is largely for *training*, and it would be a sad day when the training was lost or even minimized.

"Children can be taught to pray only by praying, and to work by working, and to express their love for Christ by expressing it in some simple, natural, childlike way; and it is still necessary and always will be necessary to devote much of the Junior hour to the prayer-meeting and much of the strength of the Junior Society to the committees—the lookout, and the social, and the flower, and the sunshine committees, and all the others which furnish the indispensable and absolutely necessary means of child-training.

"But at the same time I think that at least ten minutes of every hour might with profit be used for instruction by question and answer—where the answers should be carefully learned—concerning the great doctrines of the church, its history and purpose, and the practical concerns of daily life which result from these teachings.

"Some pastors and superintendents may deem it best to concentrate this catechetical instruction into six or eight weeks of the year instead of using ten minutes each week; that is, they will give the whole hour to catechetical training for a few weeks, and for the rest of the year to the training idea. In either case this catechism of doctrines and duties will furnish a splendid preparation for church membership, and every year an intelligent class of earnest, intelligent junior Christians may be fitted for the church.

"What a wide and important field does this open! How easily in this way may our children be taught, not only what their church believes, but what it stands for in history; something about the great men who have made its history, and something as well about the church universal and the martyrs and heroes who belong to all branches of it! How plainly can it be made to appear that right living and pure thinking and honesty and reverence and faithfulness and obedience are all connected vitally with the religion of Christ! How much the children may learn in this way that they will never forget about the cause of missions, and especially about the work which their own denomination is set to maintain in the home land and other lands!

"I think the answers to the questions should be *learned* week by week. This will bring about a revival of the too-much neglected art of memorizing Scripture passages, and important truths framed in other words as well. The Juniors usually stay in the same society three or four or five years; and during these years, if only one

question is taken up and answered and thoroughly learned
and explained each hour, a very large amount of gospel
truth can be inculcated.

"One minister to whom I have written wisely advises
that this be made a concert exercise, and that at first all
the children should be drilled to answer the question together, and that they then may be questioned upon it
separately. But all these details will be wisely managed
by the versatile and consecrated superintendents and pastors. I have consulted many pastors of all denominations concerning this plan of instruction for the Juniors,
and all are enthusiastic for it. To all who desire I can
furnish a list of over fifty catechisms used by different
denominations. Large as it is, this list is doubtless far
from complete."

In my own experience I have often found it peculiarly
helpful to take the church covenant and creed, to go
through it with the boys and girls sentence by sentence,
reducing the theological terms to their every-day equiv-
alents, and striving to bring these somewhat formidable
compendiums of belief within the reach of the child's
mind.

More than once with the boys and girls I went through
Bunyan's "Pilgrim's Progress," and found that the al-
legories of the immortal dreamer made plain to the child
of to-day the pathway from the City of Destruction to
Beulah Land.

In many churches the Junior Endeavor Society is doing
very much this work for the boys and girls all the year

round. From the ranks of these societies have come hundreds of thousands of youthful church members, trained and equipped as they would not otherwise have been. In many churches it accomplishes the object of the pastor's class and supplements his efforts in a wonderfully effective way. It always welcomes his presence and is his society to use as he chooses for the training and instruction of the boys and girls. For a part or the whole of the year, as he pleases, he can make it "the pastor's class," and in it prepare year by year a fresh company of recruits for the army of the living God.

The liturgical churches have made far more use of the catechetical method of Christian nurture than many of the free churches of America and Great Britain, and have found vast profit therein. The plan of the pastor's class is simply an adaptation of the confirmation class to the needs of all the churches which have not inherited this means of nurture from immemorial times.

When we come to other forms of work for young people I can not speak at length, as it is in my heart to do, and in words of highest commendation, of the Young Men's Christian Association; for its work, not being directly connected with the local church, does not come within the scope of this volume.

Within the Episcopal fold the Brotherhood of St. Andrew does a similar and often most important work for the young men in the local church, while the Brotherhood of Andrew and Philip is an efficient interdenominational organization which in a considerable number of churches has set young men to reach young men in the blessed work of evangelization.

There are other methods of Christian nurture which will commend themselves to certain pastors. The Boys' Brigade has been used successfully in not a few churches in teaching the boys obedience, reverence, and the soldierly qualities of discipline, as well as the distinctive truths of the Bible. An objection urged by many is that it fosters the military spirit and is often a matter of considerable expense for uniforms, toy guns, etc. Sometimes, too, there is a danger that the real spiritual purpose will be overshadowed by the military trappings, and that the religious instructor will be lost in the drill-master. Still, these evils are incidental and not inherent, and where the combination of captain and teacher is just right the results are often admirable. Boys' clubs have been useful in some places where the right leader can be found, and other similar methods should receive sympathetic attention.

Another side of the Christian character is cultivated by children's mission circles, in which the boys and girls are taught to know the work of the heroes of the mission fields and the needs of the heathen world, and to pray and give and work for those in distant lands and the home-lands who are less favored than themselves. Such circles have done admirable service in developing this side of the Christian life. As a rule, the missionary spirit can be developed more effectively in an organiza-tion like the Junior Christian Endeavor Society, which appeals to the all-round religious life of the boys and girls. These societies should always have their mission-ary department, which shall do for all what the mission circle has heretofore done for comparatively few.

The bands of King's Daughters and King's Sons, too, have done, and are doing, a most important work in training the children in habits of gentleness, kindness, and helpfulness to others; to do kind deeds every day and to do them for Christ's sake, comes very near em-bracing the whole gospel as well as the law and the prophets.

So, too, the Bands of Mercy, a most helpful effort to teach kindness to dumb animals, the Loyal Temperance Legions, and other similar organizations for children, have worked admirably along certain lines, and deserve no small credit for instilling into the hearts of our chil-dren the virtues of temperance, purity, and kindness to the animal creation.

Another chapter will attempt to show how all these most important elements in Christian training may be brought together and "domed over," as it were, under the roof of an organization that can give a large, whole-some, symmetrical training to all the moral and spiritual muscles of our growing boys and girls.

.

THE YOUNG PEOPLE'S SOCIETY OF
CHRISTIAN ENDEAVOR AS A
TRAINING-SCHOOL OF
THE CHURCH

Chapter III

THE YOUNG PEOPLE'S SOCIETY OF CHRIS-TIAN ENDEAVOR AS A TRAINING-SCHOOL OF THE CHURCH

THE HISTORY OF THIS TRAINING-SCHOOL.—WHERE THE ORIGINAL SUGGESTION CAME FROM—MANY ORIGINAL ENDEAVORERS—HOW THE CRYSTALS WERE PRECIPITATED—CHRISTIAN ENDEAVOR A UNI-FIER AND SIMPLIFIER—ONE ELEMENT LARGELY LEFT OUT OF FOR-MER ORGANIZATIONS—PERSONAL EXERCISE AND TRAINING AS IM-PORTANT AS TEACHING—A GOOD DEFINITION OF TRUE CHILDREN OF THE CHURCH—THE ANALOGY BETWEEN PHYSICAL AND SPIR-ITUAL TRAINING—EXERCISE AS NECESSARY FOR YOUNG CHRISTIANS AS FOR YOUNG HORSES—AN ANCIENT PROTOTYPE OF THE MODERN ENDEAVOR SOCIETY—COTTON MATHER'S PROPOSAL FOR "THE RE-VIVAL OF DYING RELIGION"—SOME REMARKABLE RESEMBLANCES TO MODERN METHODS—THE CURE FOR HELPLESSNESS—THE IM-PORTANCE OF NORMAL HEALTHY ACTIVITY—THE FIRST CONSTITU-TION OF THE FIRST SOCIETY—THE FIRST SOCIETY BORN IN A REVIVAL—THE OPENING OF THE FIRST CHRISTIAN ENDEAVOR FLOWER—EXPERIMENTS OF THE PAST—THE SECOND SOCIETY—CRITICS AND CRITICISMS—THE FLEXIBILITY OF THE SOCIETY—FOUR CARDINAL PRINCIPLES: CONFESSION, SERVICE, FELLOWSHIP, LOYALTY—THE PSYCHOLOGIST AND THE PRACTICAL WORKER—THE STEPPING-STONE, THE TRAINING-SCHOOL, AND THE WATCH-TOWER.

IN approaching this subject I am embarrassed by the fear that I shall be considered a special pleader for a pet project. I can not claim to regard the history or the principles of the Christian Endeavor movement with indifference, but I have tried to consider them, not in the light of my preconceived opinions, but in the light of the history and experience of twenty years, and I have tried not to read into this history my own prejudices and predilections.

No one can realize more fully than I the small part I have had in establishing this society, how largely it has been taken by Providence out of human hands, how spontaneously it has developed; and no one is more grateful that this is not a man-made scheme of Christian nurture, but a God-sent movement.

I have often been asked about the genesis of the Young People's Society of Christian Endeavor; where the original suggestion came from; with whom the name originated, and so on. Moreover, my memory has often been jogged by those who were very sure that they knew all about it. The idea originated, I am told, with any one of a hundred men who have been named. I have met at least half a hundred of the original Endeavorers from whom, according to themselves, the idea was borrowed. In fact, I have read more than one serious biography of myself in which the statement has been made that I was born in some town which as a matter of fact I have never seen, grew up in a church whose name I had never heard, and obtained the idea, afterward modified and enlarged, from some pastor whose identity had not been revealed to me until I read his letter or his article in the public press.

The fact of the matter seems to be that the Christian

Y. P. S. C. E. as Training-School of Church

Endeavor movement was crystallizing for years and needed but a little event to precipitate the crystals and give them shape. It may be fair to say that it originated with no one in particular, but with many in general. Ten thousand pastors in ten thousand churches twenty years ago felt the need of some systematic and efficient method of Christian nurture. Hundreds were experimenting along different lines, but all these lines converged at one center, a heartfelt desire to train the children and youth for God. Moreover, all these methods and experiments (some of which I have described in the last chapter) made almost inevitable some organization which should combine them and use them more effectively. There was no unity or cohesion to these plans. One little group of children was being trained in missionary activity and was being taught to think and pray and work for the heathen world. Another was being taught in temperance lore, to hate the wine-cup, and to wear proudly the blue ribbon. A few others were being trained to be kind to animals, and others were learning the Bible in the Sunday-school or the catechism in the pastor's class.

But the young people who were in one organization could not well be in another. Those who belonged to the Mission Circle did not have much time for the Band of Hope, and it was evident that some unification, arrangement, and systematization of these plans was necessary. In tens of thousands of churches this unification has been found very largely in the Christian Endeavor Society or organizations founded upon similar methods.

I do not mean that there was any set purpose to unify these different organizations. No man surely had any such purpose, but in the Providence of God it has come about that under the roof of one organization, with its different meetings and its different committees, many of these efforts for the youth have found their home. The Christian Endeavor movement unwittingly has become a great simplifier of church machinery. The same young people are taught not only temperance, but foreign missions and home missions, and philanthropic work, and not only the evil of intoxicants, but the fruits of the Spirit—to be kind and gentle, generous and manly, and to use all their powers for Christ.

It is noticeable that in these former organizations and methods of training the young people, one element was largely left out—the element of training, of personal exercise. If you will examine carefully all these plans, admirable as many of them were, you will notice that, almost without exception, the teaching element predominated. It entirely overshadowed, if it did not absolutely displace, the idea of training. In fact, it is surprising how largely this idea of training the young had been disregarded in the past. It is not unnatural, perhaps, for the past originated and lived up to the adage that "Children should be seen and not heard." The past, as compared with these last days at least, was the period of repression. Young America had not come to the front. The industrial school was unknown. A manual training class had been unheard of. Sloid was never taught in our grammar schools, and the religious instruction of our churches corresponded in its leading ideas to the secular instruction of our schools.

In the providence of God, as it seems to me, without human design or intention and with very little human wisdom, the Christian Endeavor Society came to remedy this defect and to provide the all-important element of training—to exalt it side by side with the idea of instruction in all our churches.

One of the best definitions that I have ever heard of those two modern children of the church, the Sunday-school and the Young People's Society of Christian Endeavor, is as follows: "The Sunday-school is the church instructing the young; the Christian Endeavor Society is the church training the young."

The following paragraphs were written in the very earliest days of the Christian Endeavor movement, and the force and importance of the statements have been growing upon me with every passing year. It seems to me that the spiritual training of the child lies at the very foundation of the Christian Endeavor movement as a modern means of Christian nurture.

"The analogy between the physical and spiritual training of the child is very close. We sometimes say, in the exaggeration of familiar speech, that such and such a child of indulgent parents has had everything done for him, and yet what we really mean is only this: that every facility has been provided that love and wealth can suggest to enable the child to do well for himself. The kind parent can provide good air for his child and perfect ventilation, but after all the child must breathe the air for himself. The most loving parent can not *exercise* for the child. The young person must do this for himself. Perhaps this is the most important and most neglected element of self-culture in religious matters. For invalids there are many strong advocates of the system of massage, in which the body of the sick man is pinched and pulled and kneaded and worked over; this may do very well for the invalid, who has not strength to exercise himself, but none of us would claim that massage is the best exercise for the growing child. In order to grow strong he must run, and jump, and play *for himself.*

"The cord that draws the young soul upward toward God is woven of a threefold strand. He must know what Christ's will is through the instruction of parents and Christian teachers; he must publicly acknowledge that Christ's will is his will; and then he must do that will. Instruction, confession, activity—these three elements entering into the young life, when preceded by a complete heart surrender, can not fail to develop the strong man, ' complete in Him.'

"It is just as unreasonable to expect the child to grow strong of muscle and supple of limb while strapped to a bed and never allowed to rise and run about, as to expect the young disciple to grow 'strong in the Lord' while never exercising his spiritual faculties.

Y. P. S. C. E. as Training-School of Church

"The instruction of the pulpit and Sunday-school may well be likened to the food provided at the family table. It is, very likely, abundant in quantity and nutritious in quality, but food without exercise in the family circle makes the sickly, dyspeptic child. Food without exercise in the church is apt to produce no better results.

"Even the horses in our stables can not long live without exercise. Fill their cribs never so full of the best feed, they must yet *do* something to keep healthy. This is a natural law, which is imperative in the spiritual world. There are a great many dyspeptic Christians in all our churches. They are bilious and disappointed and hopeless and useless, except as they become by their continual growling and fault-finding means of grace in the form of chastisement to the pastor and other workers. In fact, they have all the symptoms of spiritual dyspepsia. Now the only remedy for this disease is spiritual activity. ' Go to work,' said the famous English doctor to his rich, dyspeptic patient; ' go to work. Live on sixpence a day, *and earn it.* ' " *

It is interesting to notice how young people themselves have felt the need of this training, of this exercise in the Christian graces, and have reached out after it even when it was being withheld by their elders.

As the baby must kick its feet and wave its ineffectual arms if it is well and strong, as the boy and girl must romp and play and exercise their muscles whether a gymnasium is provided for them or not, so there seems to be something in the nature of the young Christian

* Clark, " Young People's Prayer-Meetings."

that demands exercise. He must do something for himself. He will be stifled and dwarfed if everything is
done for him.

The sense of this universal need is shown by the unor-
ganized groups of young people of which I have before
spoken, who used to gather together especially in times
of revival interest to pray for and encourage each other.
This sense of the need of exercise accounts for the many
young people's meetings which in former days often
died a lingering death, and were revived only to die
once more.

A notable instance of such a desire for personal religious exercise and work is shown by a movement which
began in the early part of the eighteenth century and
survived but a few years, crushed out apparently by the
indifference or hostility of the churches. This movement bore many remarkable likenesses to the modern
Society of Christian Endeavor. These young people of
nearly two hundred years ago had their weekly meeting,
in which, according to the provision of the ancient constitution, it was ordered that "there be two hours at a
time set apart, and let there be two prayers made by the
members of the society in their turns, between which let
a sermon be repeated, and there should be the singing of
a psalm annexed." This society was apparently originated by none other than the distinguished Cotton
Mather, who told about it in a little book, now very rare
and valuable, whose title-page reads:

Religious Societies.

PROPOSALS

For the *REVIVAL* of

Dying Religion,

BY WELL-ORDERED

Societies

FOR THAT PURPOSE.

With a brief DISCOURSE, Offered unto a RELIGIOUS SOCIETY, on the Firſt Day of their Meeting.

1 Theſſ. V. 11. *Edify one another*

BOSTON:
Printed by S. KNEELAND, for JOHN PHILLIPS, and Sold at his Shop over againſt the South-ſide of the Town Houſe. 1724.

This society, which I had not heard of until an antiquarian brought it to my attention years after the Christian Endeavor movement was well under way, had several other features analogous to the modern Endeavor Society. For instance, corresponding to the roll-call meeting of the modern Society of Christian Endeavor, Art. V. of Cotton Mather's manual provides:

> V. LET the Lift be once a _Quarter_ called over; and then, If it be observed, that any of the _Society_ have much absented themselves, Let there be some sent unto them, to inquire the _Reason_ of their _Absence_; and if no _Reason_ be given, but such as intimates an _Apostacy_ from good Beginnings, Let them upon obstinacy, after loving and faithful Admonitions, be _Obliterated._

Doubtless the names and not the persons were to be "obliterated," but here was the modern consecration meeting in its embryonic form and the very same means of keeping the society free from inactive members.

"It is very certain," remarks the distinguished author, "that where such Private Meetings, under a good Conduct have been kept alive, the Christians which have composed them, have like so many Coals of the Altar kept one another alive, and kept up a lively Christianity in the neighborhood. Such Societies have been tried, and proved to be strong Engines, to uphold the Power of Godliness. The throwing up of such Societies has been accompanied with a Visible Decay of Godliness. The less Love to them, the less Use of them, there has been in a Place, the less has Godliness flourished there; the less there has been of the Kingdom of God."*

* Cotton Mather, "Proposals for the Revival of Dying Religion."

Y. P. S. C. E. as Training-School of Church

It is worthy of note that these societies were started in a period of religious declension and dearth as was the Young People's Society of Christian Endeavor, for the very same purpose—to bring about decisions for Christ and training in His service.

For a time these societies multiplied, but, alas! they were not looked upon with much favor. The ecclesiastical spirit of the times was against lay activities, and especially against the activities of young and inexperienced laymen. The tithing-man was more in evidence than the lookout committee to keep the young people in the right way. The church acted the part of the traditional stepmother rather than of the loving parent to this new organization. It was soon crushed out and after a few years we hear little of it.

It is chiefly interesting to us of to-day as showing the desire ineradicable in the heart of the young Christian to do as well as to get; to give as well as to receive; to exercise as well as to be taught. This desire can not be frozen by ecclesiastical coldness or crushed by churchly indifference. It is implanted in the heart of the young Christian. It demands free scope, and in these later days has received such recognition as never before, for the whole Christian Endeavor movement in every land is based on this thought of exercise, of manifestation of life, of training as distinct from religious teaching and equally necessary with it.

The vital importance of religious activity to supplement and round out religious instruction is recognized by the psychologists as well as by the practical pastor and evangelist. It is taught by philosophy as well as by history.

"The cure for helplessness that comes with storm and stress in the period of adolescence," says Professor Starbuck, "is often found in inducing wholesome activity. 'Faith without works is dead.' Let us call to mind the fact that storm and stress and doubt are experienced some time during youth by something like seventy per cent of all the persons studied. On the other hand, heightened activity, which is characterized not only by interest in religious matters but by engaging in actual religious work, was experienced by only about twenty-two per cent of all these persons. This is doubtless very much out of proportion. Many persons have found the solution of their difficulties by actually setting about doing things."*

This is exactly what the Christian Endeavor Society seeks to do for every one of its members. It sets them about doing things and thus tides them over the critical periods of adolescence, the years of storm and stress and doubt. Professor Coe confirms Professor Starbuck in prescribing the same treatment for those who are distressed by doubts and fears. We must add to the intellectual food something not less needful:

"The youth should by all means be induced to be active in those forms of religious living that still appeal to

* Starbuck, "Psychology of Religion."

him at all. . . . Religious activity and religious comforts may abide at the same time that the intellect is uncertain how this fits into any logical structure. Thus it comes to pass that the greatest thing we can do for the doubting youth is to induce him to give free exercise to the religious instinct. Let him not say what he does not actually believe, let him not compromise himself in any way, but it is always certain that he still believes and feels and aspires enough to give him a place among religious people." *

It is just this normal, healthy, necessary activity, which the scientific psychologist recognizes as so important in the period of adolescence, that the Society of Christian Endeavor attempts to supply. The philosophy of its success, so far as the society has been successful, is that it fits the needs of the young soul. It is no haphazard experiment. Its roots run down into the nature of youth. In God's good plan the wards of the key fit the lock, and the door of larger service and nobler living is through it opened to young men and women.

The simple story of the beginning of the Christian Endeavor movement need not be rehearsed at length; it has been often enough told. The society had its humble origin in a church in the city of Portland, Me., about twenty years ago. The first society was simply an experiment of one pastor in the training of youth for Christ—such an experiment as thousands of others were making with anxious hearts, and which led these thou-

* Coe, "Spiritual Life."

sands so quickly to unite in one plan when it was presented to them.

There hangs upon a wall in my house, in a room devoted to Christian Endeavor banners, badges, and mementos from all parts of the world, a faded hectograph copy of the original constitution of the first Society of Christian Endeavor. I remember very well copying the constitution upon this hectograph pad, because it did not seem worth while to waste money and printer's ink upon a document so perishable and ephemeral. Thus the constitution was printed and distributed among the earliest members. It has since been printed, it is supposed, in at least sixty different languages, and to the extent of not less than ten millions of copies, while the pledge has been printed not less than one hundred millions of times.

I speak of this to show how little human wisdom or forethought there was in the inception of the Christian Endeavor movement. It was simply a very humble effort of a very humble pastor, but it is such seeds which God often plants and from which He grows a harvest. It is the foolishness of organizations as well as the foolishness of preaching (not foolish organizations or foolish preaching) which confounds the wise, for few of the wise men of that day saw any hope or promise in this plan of Christian nurture. In fact, many saw only something to distrust or condemn or perhaps ridicule, and not a few were the articles and the addresses which in those early days were aimed against the new society.

There are, however, some points often overlooked that are worth noting in this early history. The first Society of Christian Endeavor was born in a period of dearth and sluggishness in the church at large. For many years, as the records prove, additions to the churches were few. It was a period of unrest and inquiry and much solicitude, especially concerning the young. Every ministers' meeting was discussing the matter. The first society was the outcome of a local revival. It breathed the warm atmosphere of a religious awakening. It was an honest effort to help the young people to help themselves. It was an attempt to supply the lack of training; to balance the teaching of others with the personal work of the young converts. It was an effort to provide exercise as well as food for the soul. It was the effort of a pastor. It was an effort in the church, for the church, of the church. All the later growth of the society shows the marks of these early days. The constitution, tho enlarged and amended, is substantially the same as when drawn up and printed on that hectograph pad. Still the great object of the society is to provide a training-school for the youth. Still its purpose is to teach them to do things by doing them; not by hearing how they ought to be done. Still it is the pastor's solicitude and the pastor's joy if he uses it aright. Still it is in the church and of the church and for the church. Still it flourishes best in a warm, evangelistic atmosphere. Still its great object and purpose is to conserve the fruits of every religious awakening, and, as its constitution says, to make the young people, thus awakened, "more useful in the service of God."

With great solicitude I watched the opening of the first Christian Endeavor flower, lest it should be blighted by some untoward wind before it had fairly blossomed. Various other experiments had been tried in the Williston church to win and hold the young people, but they had largely or wholly failed of their object. The reason of their failure was because I had expected too little of the young people, because I had not appealed to the heroic in their natures, because I had thought that the young soul could be coaxed into the kingdom and satisfied with entertainments and games and "pink teas" and oyster suppers. It was a woful mistake; but one which a young pastor perhaps may be pardoned for making, since he had never been taught any better, and since a multitude of others were making the same blunders.

The Christian Endeavor Society, warned by the foolish experiments of tickling the young Christian with the straws of amusement, started out on totally different lines. The young people were not to have everything done for them, but were to do for themselves. They were not to have the way to heaven made smooth and easy; they were to overcome its obstacles and level its rough places. They were not simply to be preached at and prayed for; *they* were to speak in a manner appropriate to youth, and *they* were to pray. They were not to be excused from every duty because of some whim or mood or passing indisposition; they were to overcome their whims and control their moods and make a sacred engagement with their fellows every week to meet them in the prayer-room and do a Christian's tasks.

As the society was a radical departure from every plan that had been tried in that church, so the results obtained were strikingly different from anything before accomplished by the young people. The young people's meeting, which had been a dead-and-alive affair dependent altogether for life upon the passing waves of spiritual emotion, took on new and permanent power. Every meeting was a good one, because in every meeting the rank and file had part and exercised their spiritual graces. The monthly roll-call meeting showed who the few delinquents were, and enabled the older members and the pastor to deal with them. The committees furnished to every one some definite and appropriate work that gave them the exercise they needed to digest the truth they already knew. The monthly reports of the committees kept the members up to their duties and modestly showed their successful efforts or revealed their delinquencies. Others were brought in constantly through the associate door of the society into the active membership and into the church. In short, a constant spirit of religious enthusiasm for work and worship pervaded the society. The old order of things seemed to have passed away, and many things, at least in the lives of these young people, had become new. As the farmers say that in the hot days of August they can see the corn grow on the Western prairies, so it seemed to me that I could see these young disciples grow in grace.

The society spread quietly but rapidly from this starting-point. Eight months later the second society was formed; this one in Newburyport, Mass. A few days later another and then another was organized. The gathering snowball grew larger and larger as it rolled on, until in a few years every State and province in North America and almost every country in the world had its Christian Endeavor contingent.

Of course there were criticisms, some of them vinegarish, most of them kindly and helpful. It was said that the prayer-meeting rule would make the young people formal and perfunctory in their participation; that it would develop prigs and precocious young exhorters; that it would set them up in their own estimation above their elders; that it would separate them into cliques and clans; and that the church would lose its young life, which would thus be absorbed in a separate organization.

The answer to most of these objections was "Wait and see." In the original society the plan has not made prigs or formalists. The prayer-meeting is not a perfunctory routine service, but more vital and instinct with spiritual life than ever before. The young people are not divided

100

into disloyal cliques, but are more eager to serve the church than ever they were before. Theoretical objections do not stand before practical demonstrations. The best answer to the early critics of Christian Endeavor were the Christian Endeavor societies themselves. The best answer to-day to objections is a well-organized, thoroughgoing, genuine Society of Christian Endeavor.

Other objections were evidently founded on misapprehensions which were easily removed. At first it was supposed by many that it was expected that every immature Christian should preach a little sermon or offer a well-rounded prayer, but it soon became known that a very simple participation satisfied all the requirements of the pledge—a verse of Scripture, an appropriate quotation, a word of testimony, a sentence of prayer. This participation, it was seen, was as appropriate for the boy in the young people's meeting, as the long ten-minute prayer of his grandfather, in which the Jews were never forgotten, was appropriate to the mid-week meeting of the church. Another misapprehension was the relation of the society to the church. In those early days it was not always understood that it was not, strictly speaking, a "relation" of the church. It was and is the church, a part of the church, and the church training the young. It is the church meeting in its young people's service; the church working in its young people's committees; the church praying through the voices of its youth.

Even now it is difficult thoroughly to establish this idea. Some still seem to think that the church is the Sunday-morning service or the Sunday-evening service; that the church is the minister and the office bearers; that the church is some particular service or section of its membership; and we sometimes hear wails about disintegrating the church because the young people have their meeting and their special plans for doing a special work which the church needs to have done.

Away with this medieval idea! The church is the aggregate of its members at work in their different ways and according to their different capacities. The church is found instructing in the preaching services and the Sunday-school. The church is found praying in the prayer-meeting for young and old. The church working is the benevolent and missionary organizations and committees for both sexes and all ages. A clear apprehension of this truth, which I believe can not be gainsaid, cuts the ground from under most of the serious objections which have been made to the young people's movement.

I recently returned from my third journey around the world in the interests of the Christian Endeavor movement, and in view not of my theories and predilections, but of actual experience with societies in these many lands as well as at home, I wish to present the fundamental principles on which I believe the movement is based. If this presentation has no other merit, it is at least the result of careful observation and experience in many lands. Sometimes, perhaps, this can better be trusted in a matter of practical concern than the theories of the doctrinaire. There is a God-sent element in experience and the practise of hundreds of thousands of earnest hearts that is not always found in the study. If I can restate the principles of the Christian Endeavor movement in the terms of experience, it will be worth more than any theories or reasonings which tempt one by their originality and novelty.

One test of a truth is that it is universal. Faith is faith in India and Kamchatka. Hope is hope in the New World and the Old. Charity is the "greatest of these" at the equator and the pole. So it is in all lesser matters that have in them the elements of universal truth. Here is the test of the value of an idea, of a movement, of an organization. Is it a temporary expedient that meets some local temporary need, or is it a satisfaction for a universal need? Is it a post to which something may be tied for a little, or is it a tree, with deep-running roots and wide-arching branches, which grows with the years, and whose seed takes root in any fertile soil? Thus can movements be tested.

Let us apply this proof to the principles of the Christian Endeavor Society, and see if they meet the test.

In any such movement there must necessarily be many things that are local and temporary. Committees that are necessary in one society are entirely unnecessary in another. Place and hour of service, methods of roll-call, ways of conducting the meetings, frequency and character of business gatherings—all afford room for an infinite variety of details, preventing any dull uniformity of method, and affording opportunity for the utmost ingenuity and resourcefulness. In these details societies in different parts of the world will surely differ one from another, and they ought to do so. These matters are not the essential, universal principles of the movement. It would be the height of absurdity to say that, because a society in London has its meeting at seven o'clock Monday evening, a society in Labrador should observe the same day and hour; that because a society in Sydney has nineteen committees, a society in Shanghai must have just a score less one.

A thousand matters are left free and flexible in Christian Endeavor. Personal initiative, invention, resource, the constant leading of the Spirit of God, are possible and necessary. The Christian Endeavor constitution is no hard chrysalis which forever keeps the butterfly within from trying its wings. There is room even for experiments and failures, since we will always remember that the worst failure is to make no endeavor. Yet, while this is true, it is equally true that a universal movement must have principles that do not change with the seasons, do not melt at the tropics or congeal at the poles. A tree puts forth new leaves every year; but it does not change its roots. It simply lengthens and strengthens them. The roots of the Christian Endeavor tree, wherever it grows, are Confession of Christ, Service for Christ, Fellowship with Christ's People, and Loyalty to Christ's Church. The farther I travel and the more I see of societies in every land, the more I am convinced that these four principles are the essential and the only essential principles of the Christian Endeavor Society. Let me repeat them:

I. Confession of Christ.

II. Service for Christ.

III. Fellowship with Christ's People.

IV. Loyalty to Christ's Church.

With these roots the Christian Endeavor tree will bear fruit in any soil. Cut away any of these roots in any clime, and the tree dies.

I. *Confession of Christ* is an essential in the Christian Endeavor Society. To insure this in appropriate and natural ways, the methods of the society are adapted in every particular. Every week comes the prayer-meeting, in which every member who fulfils his vows takes some part, unless he can excuse himself to his Master. This participation is simply the confession of Christ. This confession is as acceptably made by the unlearned, stumbling, lisping Christian as by the glib and ready phrase-maker, if the few and halting words of the former have the true ring of sincerity about them.

The covenant pledge is a tried and proved device to promote frequent confession of Christ. It secures, as nothing else has been known to do, the frequent and regular confession of Christ by the young Christian. It also secures familiarity with the Word of God, by promoting Bible reading and study in preparation for every meeting. There is sometimes an outcry against the pledge, as tho we exalted a mere instrument to the place of a universal principle. This is not the case. We exalt the pledge as a builder exalts his plumb-line and spirit-level. They are not his house, but he can not build so good a house without as with them. We exalt the pledge as a painter exalts his brush, as a musician his violin, as a writer his pen. The brush is not the picture, the violin is not the music, the pen is not the poem; but the brush helps make the picture, the violin the music, the pen the poem; and the pledge helps make the Christian Endeavor Society because it insures regular and frequent confession of Christ. Let it be understood; no form of words is insisted on. Any pastor is free to make his own pledge; only let the Christian Endeavor essentials be set forth in it.

So also the consecration meeting, with its roll-call, is another instrument that makes confession doubly sure and doubly sacred. The calling of the names at the monthly roll-call declares the faithful confessor of Christ, and also reveals the careless non-confessor and pledge-breaker, and confronts each one, month by month, with the solemn question:

"Am I on the Lord's side?
Do I serve the King?"

106

This principle of confession in Christian Endeavor, I have found all the world around, is not dependent on degrees of latitude and longitude. The societies in Foochow, China, have flourished and multiplied because from the beginning they have observed this feature of Christian Endeavor. The rude little groups of Christians on the Ningpo, just out of rank, crass heathenism, have caught hold of this great principle in their societies, and, tho they have little else in common with our methods, are worthy the fellowship of any of us. In a post and telegraph station in North Japan, in the Beals of East Bengal, on the ships of the United States navy, in the prisons of Kentucky and Indiana, among the rude Islanders of the South Seas, this covenant is kept, and the Christian Endeavor Society flourishes because the covenant idea insures constant confession of Christ where nothing of the sort flourished before, for it is one of the main trunk-roots through which it draws nourishment and life.

In this virtue of free, outspoken confession of our faith, we Anglo-Saxon Protestants are singularly lacking. I know of no race that is so shamefaced about its faith, so unwilling to declare its allegiance. The Turk stands five times a day and prays with his face toward Mecca, caring not who sees him. On the housetop, by the wayside, in the courtyard of the inn, when the hour of prayer comes, he unfailingly declares: "Great is God, and Mahomet is His prophet." I have heard the

Buddhist mutter half the day long: "I believe in Buddha, I believe in Buddha." And much of the propagating power of these false or defective faiths and the tremendous hold they have on the human race to-day is the result of this unabashed, outspoken proclamation of their doctrines.

II. The second essential of the Christian Endeavor Society is constant *service for Christ*. Here, too, can we not see the hand of God in building the society on this corner-stone? For various reasons our churches have come to contain many silent partners, many who do not serve. Social consideration, decline of early zeal, physical incapacity, have filled our church rolls and have not multiplied our church workers. I am not finding fault or indulging in a cheap fling at the laziness of Christians. This is simply a fact. Some counteracting forces were needed. Here is one of them— a society whose ideal, like Wesley's, is, "At it, and all at it, and always at it "—a society that finds a task for the least as well as the greatest, for the youngest and most diffident as well as for the few natural-born leaders.

III. Again, it is plain that *fellowship* is an essential feature of the Christian Endeavor movement. This, too, is not a matter of zones, or climates, or latitudes, or languages. This fellowship is a universal, God-given, fundamental feature of Christian Endeavor. In every land I have felt the heart-throbs of my fellow Christians.

This fellowship is expressed in different ways, but it is always the same fellowship.

In Japan, I have prostrated myself on hands and knees with my fellow Endeavorers and touched my forehead to the floor as they touched theirs.

In China, over and over again, a thousand Endeavorers have stood up as I addressed them, and have shaken their own hands at me while I have shaken mine at them.

In India they have hung scores of garlands about my neck, until I have blushed for my own unworthiness of such a flowery welcome.

In Bohemia they have embraced me and kissed me on either cheek (the aged *fathers* of the church, it should be understood, indulge in this salutation).

In Mexico they have hugged me in a bear's embrace, and patted me lovingly on the back.

Always it has been evident that these greetings were far more than personal matters. They represent the fellowship of the cause. Always, whatever the form, the loving greeting of loving hearts is the same.

In the Fukien province of China, when we approached a Christian village—where, by the way, there is very likely to be a Christian Endeavor Society—we were sure to hear, in the soft accent of the almond-eyed peoples, the greeting, "Ping 'ang, ping 'ang, ping 'ang " ("Peace, peace, peace "). Perhaps a hundred people, old and young, would utter this benediction as we walked through a single village. So it seems to me, as I have gone around the world again and again, I have heard the gentle word of fellowship from a million Endeavorers, "Peace, peace, peace."

This fellowship is not an accident or a matter of chance. It is an inevitable result of the movement. When the second society was formed, twenty years ago, the fellowship began. Then it became inter-denominational, inter-state, inter-national, inter-racial, inter-continental, and, as some one has suggested, since

"Part of the hosts have crossed the flood,
And part are crossing now,"

it has become inter-mundane.

IV. Once more, a universal essential of the Society of Christian Endeavor is *fidelity to Christ*, to its own church, and the work of that church. It is a thoroughly evangelical movement, defining evangelical as personal faith in the divine human person and atoning work of our Lord and Savior Jesus Christ as the only and sufficient source of salvation. It does not and can not exist for itself. When it does, it ceases to be a Society of Christian Endeavor. It may unworthily bear the name. It may be reckoned in the lists, just as an unworthy man may find his name on the church roll. But a true Society of Christian Endeavor must live for Christ and the church. Its confession of love is for Christ the head; its service is for the church, His bride; its fellowship is possible only because its loyalty is unquestioned. This

110

characteristic, too, I have found as universal as the society. I have found no real exceptions. In city or country, in Christian land or mission field, in Europe, Asia, Africa, or America, it is everywhere the same.

Because these ideals and principles are held, it is sometimes necessary to urge older Christians, however, not to hold Christian Endeavorers responsible, as some are inclined to do, for every weakness among young Christians, which the society is doing its best to remedy but can not wholly overcome. Because many young people do not go to church, the society is often blamed. Because some forget their vows, the splendid fidelity of the rank and file is forgotten. Because the church pews are not filled, or the Sunday-school enlarged, or the longed-for revival comes not, the society is made the scapegoat by some unthinking Christians for these defects, for the very reason that its ideals on these matters are exalted. Each of these principles is natural and basal. No one of them is a matter of mechanism. No one is a matter of expediency. Each is a *sine qua non.* In every continent you will find these features of Christian Endeavor are necessary. You will find, also, I believe, that no other roots are vital to the tree.

These principles will be found to be as logical and as philosophical as they are practical. They are not only attested by the history of twenty years; they are thoroughly in accord with the latest researches of the scientific man who has studied the soul of the child. He

111

says: "The period of youth is incomparably the most important of all." The Christian Endeavor Society says: "I will do my best to mold and form and transform the youth."

The psychologist says: "At adolescence the spirit as well as the mind and body grows with marvelous rapidity. Then the soul opens to the eternal; then, if ever, conversion will occur."

This young people's movement says: "All my efforts shall be concentrated upon making plain to the adolescent the way into the kingdom of God, and fixing in his life habits of rational confession of Christ and faithful service of Christ."

The modern psychologist says: "The cure for the spiritual diseases of youth, which are as inevitable as measles and chickenpox, and, alas! far more lasting in their effects and often fatally destructive to a wholesome religious life, is found in inducing wholesome activity."

The Young People's Society says: "I will bend all my energies and use all my wits and resources to provide just such natural, wholesome, religious activity."

A society thus organized and based upon these principles serves the church in three distinct ways: It is a stepping-stone to the church, a training-school in the church, and a watch-tower for the church and pastor.

As a stepping-stone to the church it often bridges the dangerous gap between conversion and church membership. In some denominations quite an interval here is allowed to elapse. It is thought that children, at least, must be tested to see whether their new-found faith and hope is a passing emotion or an enduring life purpose. One of the most dangerous periods for any young Christian is this period of waiting to declare to the world his purpose. Especially is this true in churches where there is no particular provision made for probationers.

The young convert before church membership is really a probationer, and everything should be done to establish him in the faith, to develop his Christian character, and to insure the beginning of Christian activity. The mortar sets very rapidly in these early days. The whole bent and trend of the Christian life for fifty years are often determined in the first fifty days after conversion. If the young person begins his Christian life as an outspoken confessor of Christ, as an earnest worker in some branch of the church, if he begins by forming habits of prayer and Bible-reading and church loyalty, these practises will become fixed, the blessed influence of good habit — which, thank God, is as strong as bad habit—will come to the rescue, and throughout all his years his Christian life will show the impress of its earliest days.

This is exactly what the Society of Christian Endeavor attempts to do for its members who have just entered upon the Christian life. It at once takes them into

8   113

its warm embrace. It at once gives them a confession to make and a work to do. It at once surrounds them with congenial young friends who are walking the same road Zion-ward. It enables them to take the first step toward full church membership. To be sure, some churches require that none but church members shall be active members of the young people's society. Some do not think that this is invariably a good rule, but it makes little practical difference, for the young convert, tho not an active member, can come very speedily into some relation to the society; can there make some confession and do some work for his Lord.

In the second place, such a society is a training-school within the church; I do not need to dwell further upon this point, since the importance of training as distinct from teaching has already been discussed. I would simply call attention to the many ways of training which are provided in the society—training in public prayer and confession of the very simplest but yet sincerest sort; training in work for others on the lookout and social committees; training in preparation for the prayer-meeting on the prayer-meeting committee; training in temperance and missionary zeal and different sorts of Sunday-school work, and such humble ministrations as obtaining flowers for the pulpit and comforts for the sick, and running on errands for the pastor—all of which are embraced in the multifarious committees of many societies. In fact, the possibilities of the society as a training-school are only limited by the ingenuity of the pastor and the time and capacity of the members.

In the third place, as a watch-tower for the church the society serves a most important purpose. Through this agency the church may know the religious status of each one of its young people. The monthly roll-call meeting, which is almost a universal feature in these societies, is a great help in this direction, for thus, at least once a month, the pastor can hear his young Christians, called by name, renew their allegiance to their Lord in some simple and appropriate way; or, if they are derelict to this self-imposed duty, he can find out the cause of their unfaithfulness. The lookout committee may be of very great assistance to the pastor in this direction, keeping him posted concerning the members of the society and giving him the clue to the religious life of many of the young people of which he would otherwise know but little.

As a pastor I felt that none could slip away from the outward performance of duty which usually precedes or accompanies inward unfaithfulness, without my knowledge of the fact. I felt in a certain sense as tho I stood with my hands on the shoulders of each of the hundred active members of my young people's society, and that no one of them could escape that friendly grasp without my knowledge.

Thousands of pastors have assured me that their experience was the same, and I believe it is not too much to say that any society in which a pastor takes a constant and affectionate interest will prove to be his watch-tower, his training-school, as well as pathway for a multitude of youth into all church activities.

OTHER TRAINING CLASSES IN THE CHRISTIAN ENDEAVOR SOCIETY

Chapter IV

OTHER TRAINING CLASSES IN THE CHRISTIAN ENDEAVOR SOCIETY

THE TWO FOCI—THE OLD IDEA OF THE PRAYER-MEETING—EDIFI-
CATION VERSUS PRACTISE—SETTING YOUNG PEOPLE AT WORK—
THE ESSENCE OF THE PLEDGE—LATER DEVELOPMENTS OF THE
SOCIETY—ITS CONVENTIONS—THE MISSIONARY IDEA—THE JUNIOR
SOCIETY—THE QUIET HOUR—BIBLE STUDY—PHILANTHROPIC EF-
FORT—FLOATING SOCIETIES—PRISON WORK—VARIOUS FORMS OF
ACTIVITY—ORGANIZED EFFORT: NATIONAL, STATE, AND LOCAL—
MORE ABOUT JUNIOR SOCIETIES — INTERMEDIATE SOCIETIES — A
NATURAL EVOLUTION — CAUSES OF PARTIAL FAILURE — OBJEC-
TIONS—CUTTING THE CHURCH TO PIECES—HOW UNITY IS PRO-
MOTED THROUGH THE SOCIETY—OBJECTIONS TO THE PRAYER-
MEETING AND THE PLEDGE — LARGER COOPERATION — THE
NATIONS AND THE DENOMINATIONS—HOW THE SOCIETY PROMOTES
DEMOCRACY — FIVE THINGS A DENOMINATION MUST DO TO BE
SAVED—ACTUAL STATISTICS—AN APPEAL TO BROTHER MINISTERS.

LET us see how these principles are wrought out in
practise. It was seen that the distinctive features of the
Christian Endeavor movement clustered naturally about
two foci, the prayer-meeting and the committees, and
yet these two foci are really only one, for they are both
different forms of Christian activity. Confession of
Christ is one form and a most important form of Christian
service. Service along the lines of the different committees is at the same time confession that one is Christ's

119

and is trying to do His will. But for the sake of convenience it may be well to consider for a few moments these two forms of activity separately.

It must be admitted at the outset that the young people's meeting, based on the prayer-meeting pledge which requires some participation from all, is a radical departure from the old prayer-meeting idea. Most of the objections to the modern young people's prayer-meeting and to the covenant pledge which is its backbone and chief support, have come because this is not understood. The old-fashioned idea of the prayer-meeting has been imported into the new-fashioned prayer-meeting, and the old wine does not agree with the new bottles.

The old prayer-meeting idea is the idea of instruction, of "edification." It is really a continuation by the pastor and two or three gifted laymen, of the Sunday preaching service. The one test imposed upon those who take part is, "Can he speak to edification?"—not will he receive benefit from the service, but will he instruct, arouse, and stimulate others? The result of this idea is well known. In some churches the prayer-meeting became simply a lecture. The minister prepared another sermon, a little less elaborate, perhaps, and with a little less care than the Sunday sermon, and delivered it usually to a very few of the saints on a Wednesday or a Thursday evening. In most churches he was assisted by two or three or half a dozen of those who, it was thought, could "edify" the brethren. They were often the glib and the ready, but not always the profound or the most earnest.

The young people's meeting of modern times is based on a wholly different principle. Its primary thought is not instruction of others but confession of Christ by all. The young convert does not say, "I will speak if I have something interesting or eloquent to say," but, "I will speak, however trembling and hesitating and commonplace my word, because it is my confession of love to my Lord; if I have no word of my own to speak I will use the words of another which express my feelings. I will find in the Scriptures a verse that declares my love. Tho I can not offer a long and eloquent prayer I have a desire for a blessing, and to this I will give voice in a single sentence. No one will be instructed, perhaps, by what I have to say or be any the wiser from a literary or theologic standpoint, but I am at least willing they should know that I am a disciple, and I can at least open my Bible and bring to the meeting a draught from the wells of salvation."

That is the idea which underlies the modern young people's meeting and which has made it such a radical departure from the prayer-meeting of the past as carried on in most churches. I am not decrying the old prayer-meeting. It had its place and perhaps still has its place, in many churches, but I do say that there is need and urgent need of the new prayer-meeting, the prayer-meeting in which all may participate; the prayer-meeting whose chief idea is not to instruct somebody else, but to gain strength to one's own soul and give help to others by the simplest forms of confession of Christ.

The idea of instruction and edification came very near capturing the young people's prayer-meeting. In fact, the old-fashioned young people's prayer-meeting was simply a weak and limp duplicate of the other prayer-meeting of the church. It has been described, not unjustly, in these words:

"The notice was given from the pulpit that the young people's meeting would be held at the usual hour. When the usual hour arrived it required a great stretch of courtesy and an extensive winking at gray hairs and wrinkles to consider the majority of those present any longer 'young people' except by brevet. The one warm spot in the room was often the air-tight stove. One of the more elderly young men usually occupied the chair. By no possibility was it a young woman, and there were many most excruciating pauses which could only be filled up by a frequent resort to the overworked hymn-book."

I am far from saying that all young people's meetings are accurately described in the foregoing paragraph, but I can call a multitude of witnesses to testify that a great many young people's meetings could thus be described without a particle of exaggeration. Very evidently there was a fault somewhere, and I do not hesitate to say that fault lay at the very basis of the prayer-meeting idea for young people in many churches. For generations the idea of "edification" was the fetish of the young people's prayer-meeting. It came near being its utter ruin. No one was expected to take part who could not "speak to edification," and the remains of this idea, frayed and torn as they are, are still the bane of many a prayer-meeting in all parts of the world. The result has been that the prayer-meeting has fallen often into the hands of the long-winded, who have a gift at sermonizing, or who fancy they have, or into the hands of the hobby-rider, and with all its efforts after edification it has been neither edifying, instructive, nor stimulating.

The Society of Christian Endeavor started with another conception of the young people's prayer-meeting. It was a place for practise rather than for preaching; for inspiration and fellowship rather than for instruction; a place for the participation of the average two-talent people rather than of the exceptional ten-talent man and woman. Of course the idea of instruction is not to be ignored in training Christian character, but it was felt that in the preaching service, the Sunday-school, the pastor's class, the mid-week meeting of the church, instruction had its full share; and practise, training, and inspiration might claim the young people's meeting.

Moreover, to young people, at least the latter meeting proved the most truly " edifying," tho there was not a single long speech and not an attempt at eloquence. The fifty or sixty or seventy with their Scripture verses, their simple thought about the subject, and their sentence-long prayers, really seemed to edify more than extended dissertations and elaborate prayers.

The other distinctive forms of the society, as I have said, is the committees, whose purpose it is to give every member, however young and inexperienced, some definite and appropriate task. This is no easy undertaking. Few churches have ever been organized minutely or systematically. The principle of natural selection, not to say the survival of the fittest, has had full play in most of our churches. Those were allowed to do the church work who had peculiar adaptabilities for it, who had special consecration, and who were not hampered by bashfulness or diffidence. The work of the church was in as few hands as the prayer-meeting of old. Many strong churches could, and can to-day, count their real workers upon the fingers of two hands—many churches reputed strong, I should say, for I do not believe that any church whose work is done by one-tenth or one-fortieth of its members is really a vigorous church.

The Sunday-school did much to remedy this state of affairs by affording opportunity for a band of devoted men and women to instruct the children. The ladies' societies for home and foreign work utilized more of the talent of the church, but there was still little given the rank and file of the young people to do. The society of Christian Endeavor set itself seriously to this task, and I think may be said in a measurable degree to have accomplished it by giving every member something definite, appropriate, and fitted to his years to do for Christ.

Of course I do not claim for it perfection or that it has fully accomplished this most serious task, but that it has made an honest attempt in this direction, and that it has set millions of young people at some definite Christian work who otherwise would not have found their sphere, is not an empty boast.

The covenant pledge, which has been such an important and prominent feature in the history of the Christian Endeavor movement, has this for its purpose: To help every one to *serve*. The essence of it is really all in its first clause: "Trusting in the Lord Jesus Christ for strength, I promise Him that I will strive to do whatever He would like to have me do." The rest is but an amplification of this phrase.

The young Christian believes that his Lord would like to have him spend some time daily in prayer and Bible reading; that he would like to have him be loyal to his church duties; that he would like to have him confess his name before men in natural phrase and in appropriate places; that he would like to have him do appropriate work along the lines of church activity—these things the active member of the society promises to do, at the same time always putting the proviso into his covenant, "Unless prevented by a reason which I can conscientiously give to the Master." If at any special time he believes his Lord would not have him do these things, he is absolved from his promise, but he seeks no lesser excuse. When the pledge is thoroughly understood I believe that most of its objections will disappear. It is said by some to put a premium upon the expression of religious life, but this expression is so simple and natural, it is so well guarded in various ways, that it can be no burden to the earnest, conscientious soul. Besides, this is only one form of Christian activity, and it is so recognized in the pledge; it is *one* of the things which Christ would have His followers do, confess Him before men, but the pledge applies to the Christian life and to the duties of the church with equal solemnity. I do not believe, when the pledge is understood and analyzed, and especially when its workings are seen under natural conditions, that it can be objected to by any reasonable Christian worker. But, as I have before said, no form of words is obligatory. Every pastor is at liberty to make his own pledge, if he keeps to the essentials, for the one fundamental idea of the movement is that the society is to be and do what its church wishes.

The later developments of the Christian Endeavor movement are all the natural outgrowth of the ideas implanted in the first society. It is interesting to see how entirely natural, almost inevitable, these developments have been.

I. Its conventions. The society soon made its way into churches of various denominations. Some ecclesiastics in two or three denominations took alarm and

126

tried to crush the movement out of their own churches. They only partially succeeded, however, and the fellowship continued to grow, until twenty, thirty, fifty denominations were embraced in the ever-widening circle.

Then what was more natural than that alliances of friendship and fellowship should spring up between those who were bound together with so many ties of common methods of service? At once there arose a demand for an expression of this fellowship. This has been satisfied in large part by the different conventions, national, State, and local, which have been such a conspicuous and remarkable feature of the religious life of the young in these later days. There was no prearranged purpose to establish this fellowship or to promote these overwhelming gatherings of young Christians, where from twenty to sixty thousand every year come together. They came because the movement had come; unpredicted and unplanned they came, because God's time had come to enlarge the fellowship of young Christians and to lead them to know each other better and thus to love each other better.

But the movement was not confined to American churches; it soon found its way across the sea and established itself thoroughly in Great Britain and Australia, in China, India, and Continental Europe, so that there came about naturally and also inevitably an *international* relationship which promises to have results as blessed and fruitful as the interdenominational fellowship. Not only will the unseemly barriers of denominational jealousy and distrust be broken down; not only will the barbs be taken off the wire fences of sectarianism; but through the fellowship and intermingling of the young people of different lands who are bound together by the same methods of work and the same inspirations to service, there will come a new international federation of Christians; glad hands will be given across the sea, and efforts for peace and arbitration among the nations, and for the spread of the Kingdom of our Lord, will be advanced as they could not be were it not for this new bond of international fellowship.

II. Another natural outcome of the movement has been the emphasis laid upon the missionary idea. This new sense of brotherhood and comradeship brought with it a new sense of responsibility for those in darker lands than our own. The very fact that there were Endeavorers by the thousands in India and China, led the young people in America to think of the millions in these lands who were not Christians, as well as to pray for their comrades there. A wonderful impetus to the missionary thought has thus been given. "We, too, have brothers and sisters in Christian Endeavor," the young people have reasoned, "on the other side of the globe—brothers and sisters with almond eyes and yellow skins or brown skins as the case may be, in strange garb and using a strange language, but brothers and sisters nevertheless." Every convention for years has rung with the missionary motive, and multitudes of young hearts have been fired with the missionary spirit.

Two particular ways of making concrete and definite the missionary idea, called the *Tenth Legion* and the *Macedonian Phalanx*, are now established features of the Christian Endeavor movement. These names may sound fanciful, but the thing for which they stand is by no means fanciful. The "Tenth Legion," a name reminiscent of Caesar's invincible Tenth Legion, stands for those who feel it their duty to give one-tenth of their income for the advancement of the Lord's Kingdom. The "Macedonian Phalanx" for those who have heard the Macedonian cry and have resolved to go over and help their brothers, and who support, either as societies or individuals, some one on the mission field, home or foreign, to which they can not go themselves. In this manner a great many missionaries, native workers, Bible women, students, and orphans are supported by Christian Endeavorers who belong to the Phalanx of Christian givers.

It is known that in some single years more than $200,000 have been given through the denominational boards by about one-fifth of the Endeavor societies, which have reported this matter, and that this is largely an "extra asset" of missions is proved by the fact that the gifts from young people's sources have increased by just about this amount over what was given a few years ago, while in the same denominations the gifts from other sources for missions have not appreciably increased. It

9 129

is altogether probable that, if all the returns could be obtained, it would be found that more than one million dollars are given every year for mission and parochial purposes by the Christian Endeavor societies of America alone.

III. But the young people have grown older during these twenty years. Many young men who began as boys in the Junior society have come to years of manhood. They can cast their ballot for the rulers of their choice. They can have a voice in political affairs. Their religion led them to see that they had a duty to the State as well as to the church; that the caucus had a call upon them as well as the prayer-meeting; that they could not be good Christians unless they were good citizens. So inevitably this quickening religious life and consciousness of numbers, which came with the establishment of the societies on a large scale, led to the quickening of the civic conscientiousness as well. These ideas of good citizenship, too, have been greatly promoted and encouraged in the great conventions. Ten thousand hearts have been set on fire by a single ringing address to win the country for Christ, and the young men have come to see that their Christian Endeavor pledge has something to do with hostility to bossism in politics, to the unspeakable iniquities of the Tammany régime, to the wickedness in lesser cities which is smaller only because the cities are smaller than the metropolis, and the slogan of Christian citizenship and civic righteousness has sounded out a note which, I believe, will never call a retreat. The "Christian Endeavor Civic Club" is the latest embodiment of this idea.

Again we see that this is no strange graft budded on the Christian Endeavor tree; it is no abnormal idea fastened upon it as the French fastened paper cherry blossoms on their oak-trees to welcome the Czar in November, but it is the entirely natural, if not inevitable, outgrowth of the original impulse to a larger, more consecrated, and more active Christian life.

IV. Another entirely natural development of the society is called "The Quiet Hour." Millions of Christian Endeavorers, not less than ten millions all told, probably, have promised during these twenty years to pray and read the Bible every day. But it was very soon seen that, valuable, nay, indispensable as it is to Christian growth to form the habit of prayer and Bible reading, tho the habit of devotion tided the soul over from a time of drought to one of blessing, yet the kind and quality of prayer and Bible reading were most important.

Perfunctory, routine prayers are not sufficient to satisfy the ardent young soul, and when the suggestion was made that he should spend some moments every day in quietness and contemplation, that he should have a Quiet Hour with his God, and strive to win back what has been called the "lost art of contemplation," thousands and thousands eagerly seized upon the thought and enrolled themselves as "Comrades of the Quiet Hour." The importance of this feature of the Christian Endeavor society can not be measured by the tens of thousands in its enrolment, for the idea has entered into the very life of the movement. No convention is complete without its still hour of devotion and communion, and the whole organization in every land has been quieted, uplifted, and spiritualized by this thought which has so naturally and inevitably developed itself in these later years.

This phase of the movement has given birth to much devotional literature. It has introduced young people to such writers as Andrew Murray and F. B. Meyer and Handley Moule and Cuthbert Hall, and many others of like spirit among modern writers, and has brought to the attention of many young readers, who otherwise would not have made their acquaintance, such ancient classics of the Quiet Hour as Thomas à Kempis, John Tauler, Andrew Fuller, and Jeremy Taylor. It has reared some bulwarks at least against the encroaching tide of commercialism and materialism, and has led many to train their eyes upon the stars, and to see that there are worlds of spiritual experiences which can only be seen with the compound telescope of faith and meditation.

I should like to share with my hearers a few of the thousands of letters that have come to my desk within the last three years from young people who have learned the blessed secret of rational contemplation. Many of these letters are full of a rapturous joy that such an unknown continent has been discovered; that the veil has been lifted between them and the heavenlies, and that it was possible for them as well as the saints of old to "practise the presence of God."

V. But Bible reading as well as prayer has always been a feature of the Christian Endeavor movement from its earliest day to the present. The *habit* of daily Bible reading I believe to be invaluable to every young Christian, even tho there may be months or years when the deeper truths of the Word are hidden and its full meaning is not revealed to the hasty or preoccupied reader. Familiarity with the mere shell in which the Spirit has hidden the divine truth, is of great worth. But the earnest young soul is not long content with the words of Scripture; he will soon want to know its hidden meaning; he will desire to get at the heart of the gospel. And so Bible reading has led to Bible study, and Bible study often to a search for the deep things of God. Union Bible-study classes have been formed in many places, and many individual societies have added this feature to their work, while a great number have followed courses of individual Bible study that did not demand union work. It is known that one course for reading the Bible through in a year, intelligently and thoughtfully, prepared by a wise and enthusiastic Bible student,* enlisted more than ten thousand pupils in one year, while every succeeding year it has been followed by many others in different parts of the world.

* Prof. A. R. Wells.

133

VI. It can not be supposed that so many tens of thousands of eager and devoted young Christians could be banded together for worship and religious service without having their hearts stirred by the miseries and needs of others. One would expect in advance that the philanthropic spirit would early be developed, and one is not disappointed as he traces the history of the society. Many of these efforts to relieve the distress of mankind have been expended upon the local community; the young people have striven to do "ye nexte thinge." The principle of the society from the beginning has been of such loyalty to the local church that first of all the charities, benevolences, and philanthropic work of the church have engaged the attention of the members. But some organized efforts for less-favored classes outside of their own church circle have also been undertaken. And this too has all come about in a most natural and simple way. Years ago a so-called "Floating Society of Christian Endeavor" was formed upon one of the ships of the United States Navy; a few godly young sailors came together and organized themselves into such a society. The idea was as taking on the sea as on the land. And at the world's convention in London, Secretary Baer was enabled to report one hundred and twenty-three of these societies.

The thought of their brothers on the sea roused the young people on the shore to pray and labor for the sailors, and many have been the libraries and boxes of comfort-bags which have been sent to Jack Tar in consequence. An interesting illustration of the value of "floating" Christian Endeavor may be found in Nagasaki, Japan. Going ashore at the quay one is confronted by a substantial and commodious building over whose door is the sign, "Christian Endeavor Seamen's Home."

It seems that, a few years ago, the cruiser *Charleston* of the United States Navy was lying for several weeks in the harbor of Nagasaki. On the *Charleston* was a flourishing society of Christian Endeavor. These Christian Jack Tars found that there was no decent place in that great city where a sailor could obtain a meal or a night's lodging. The city was full of brothels, but had no decent cheap lodging-house. They resolved to remedy the evil. They mortgaged their own poor wages for several months, and raised six hundred dollars among themselves. Then they appealed for outside help in Nagasaki, and now they have a property worth ten thousand dollars where every year thousands of soldiers and sailors are cared for, and find a decent place of entertainment when on shore.

A somewhat similar work has been done along our stormy coasts for the brave men of the life-saving stations, among whom also a number of societies have been established.

But the most interesting and extensive work of this sort perhaps is that done in the prisons throughout the country. More than a dozen years ago the first prison

society of Christian Endeavor in America was started in
the Penitentiary of Wisconsin, and one of the most pathetic messages ever received at a convention was sent to
the great international meeting in St. Louis, which read:
"The boys in the only society in the world who can not
be represented at your meeting if they would, send
greeting."

The chaplain and the warden reported that the society
did admirable work in the prison; that discipline was
easier and the standard of conduct among the men was
raised; and that the active members had given genuine
evidence of conversion, as their future lives have witnessed.

The experiment was so successful that it was tried in
other prisons and reformatories with equally good results, and it is now supposed that there are at least two
thousand active members of Christian Endeavor societies in prisons who have given good evidence of conversion and reformation since they have entered the barred
gate.

Of course these facts have aroused great interest among
Endeavorers who live near these prisons. Different
State unions have taken up the prison work as part of
their organized effort. It is difficult to tell whether the
young people outside have done more for the prisoner
in giving him heart and hope by their kind remembrances and frequent meetings, or whether the prisoner
has done more for the young people by awakening their

interest in the unfortunate and erring, and unsealing the fountains of human kindness and brotherhood.

VII. In the following list of things actually done by the societies in different parts of the country, as culled from thousands of letters received in a single year and presented by Secretary Baer at one of the conventions, it will be seen how multifarious are the efforts of the young people and how often their hearts are stirred to philanthropic efforts by the wants and woes of others. It is published in this connection not so much to show what has been done, as to furnish suggestions of what may be done:

"Our good-literature committee has sent books and Bibles to the sailors and soldiers, to hospitals and prisons."

"Kept three children in school in Oregon who could not otherwise have gone."

"Held gospel meetings in prisons, almshouses, hospitals, old people's homes, car-stations, engine-houses, and wharves."

"Furnished dinners to the deserving poor at Christmas and Thanksgiving."

"Sent a poor family to the country for one week of fresh air."

"Distributed invitations to church in hotels and boarding-houses."

"Purchased hymn-books, libraries, church organs, and all kinds of furniture for the church."

"Assisted in conducting the Sunday-evening service, in many cases taking entire charge."

"We give one night every two weeks for work in a mission in the slum district of our city, and go four miles every Sunday afternoon to assist in the evangelistic service in the jail."

"Our ' fresh air ' committee arranged eleven picnics, sending seven hundred and seventy-nine persons into the country, our society contributing one hundred and fifty-two dollars to carry on the work in addition to supplying all the refreshments."

"Taken an active part in the local fight against the saloon."

"Organized, conduct, and support mission Sunday-schools in neglected districts in city and country."

"Clothed twenty-eight children, thus securing them as regular members for our Sunday-school."

"Conduct meetings at the Seamen's Bethel three nights in the month."

"Furnish a choir for the mid-week prayer-meeting."

"Are responsible for a chorus choir for the Sunday-evening service."

"Our Junior society gave a concert at the old ladies' home."

"Publish a church calendar and conduct our church paper."

"Our entire Junior society has organized itself into a committee for the prevention of cruelty to animals."

"Conduct a weekly prayer-meeting for ' shut-ins.' "

"Sent comfort-bags to sailors and soldiers."

"Conduct evangelistic meetings among the soldiers in camp."

"Support a pupil in a mission school."

"For ten years have had charge of a special service at the old ladies' home."

138

"Bought a new carpet for our church."

"Secured volunteer nurses for our relief-committee work."

"Paid off our church debt."

These various forms of activity—and they might be multiplied a thousandfold—show by actual practical examples what the young people can do and are glad to do when their hearts are touched by the Spirit of God and when in their organized capacity they are called upon to put their principles of service into practise.

Most useful in carrying out these special philanthropic and evangelistic efforts, as well as for binding the societies together in genuine and delightful fellowship, have been the unions, local, district, State, and national. These are no arbitrary divisions, but are the natural and inevitable expressions of the inward fellowship. The development of the local Christian Endeavor Union was natural and spontaneous. The first Union was started in New Haven, Conn., after a number of societies had been formed in that university city and some expression of their fellowship was needed.

In many country regions the plans adopted by the city union are not available, and so different plans for District unions or County unions came into vogue where they were needed.

The States form a natural unit of religious effort as well as for political legislation and government, and every State soon had its Christian Endeavor union whose conventions are often superlative in size and interest, like the recent Pennsylvania convention of 1900 which registered more than seventeen thousand delegates.

The national union is called the United Society of Christian Endeavor. Its executive offices are in Boston, and its governing body is a board of trustees, numbering about one hundred and consisting of leaders of the different denominations, who are chosen in proportion to the number of societies in these different denominations, together with the State and provincial presidents as *ex officio* members of the board. The United Society is in no sense a legislative body. It does not control any local society in any part of the world. It levies no taxes and demands no allegiance, but simply exists to promote the fellowship and efficiency of the society. Its platform of principles has been affirmed and endorsed by more than one international convention.

JUNIOR SOCIETIES

It will be seen that most of the work hitherto outlined is for the young men and maidens rather than for the boys and girls, and yet in the first society we saw that there were boys and girls as well as their older brothers and sisters. It soon became evident that a distinction in age should be made, and that the training of the children required somewhat different methods from the training of young men and women. The same principles would apply, should be applied, in a different way.

140

Other Training Classes

Moreover, it has been found that in most cases it was better to have a separate meeting for the boys and girls under fourteen or fifteen, where they would not be overshadowed by the young men and women, and where they would have more time and opportunity to take their part in the meetings and do their share of the work of the committees. It was also seen that these younger members needed more instruction and more guidance in the work that was given them to do.

So again, naturally and inevitably, without previous planning or human foresight, the Junior Christian Endeavor societies arose in response to a definite Providential call. They came because they were needed in a multitude of churches, and for that reason they have grown naturally, healthfully, rapidly. The same underlying principles apply as in the young people's societies, but they are adapted to the children's needs with all the flexibility which is so characteristic of the Christian Endeavor society.

These boys and girls, if they are Christians, are expected, as well as their older brothers and sisters, to confess Christ and work for Him, but it is a confession and a service which are entirely adapted to their years and powers. The Junior pledge for active members, which is a very simple, yet responsible, one, and the Junior pledge for preparatory members, which is still simpler, and one which any child in the world can take, read as follows:

THE JUNIOR PLEDGE FOR ACTIVE MEMBERS.

THE JUNIOR PLEDGE FOR PREPARATORY MEMBERS.

Other Training Classes

Some older person always superintends the Junior society, and upon his or her tact, winsomeness, consecration, and persistence largely depends the success of the society. It is a splendid tribute to ten thousand wise and devoted Junior superintendents that the societies of children have for so many years accomplished an increasingly fruitful work. Some Junior societies have, to be sure, died for lack of a superintendent or because his courage or devotion gave way, but most have lived and gone on from strength to strength.

Of late years another division has proved necessary in large churches. It is called the Intermediate Society of Christian Endeavor. As the Junior society takes in young persons under fourteen years of age, and as those between fourteen and eighteen or nineteen are not able always to get their full share of training in worship and service where there are many older and more experienced members present, the Intermediate societies have come to fill a real need. They are as natural and as needed as an Intermediate department in a large Sunday-school, and, just as there are Primary, Intermediate, and Senior departments in well-organized Sunday-schools where the numbers are sufficient, so there is room for all these departments of the young people's society. There is, in fact, one church in Philadelphia, the celebrated Grace Baptist Temple, that has no less than fifteen societies of Christian Endeavor for all ages, from the gray-haired grandmother to the little flaxen-haired grand-daughter, and, through this agency applying its flexible principles as may be necessary, all find a chance to express their love for Christ in words and in deeds.

I desire to have it noticed that these different outgrowths and features of the Christian Endeavor movement are genuine natural growths and not sporadic flowers or fruits. They could not have been prevented unless the movement itself was crushed and throttled as it has been in some cases by denominational zealots. From beginning to end it has had a natural, necessary development. The evolution has been entirely orderly. Christian growth has not been attempted by any patent sleight-of-hand methods. The theories of the doctrinaire have not been foisted upon the society, and I know of no one who has successfully attempted to use it for selfish purposes or to advance his own ends. Such attempts have been made, but they have met with speedy and ignominious failure. It seems to have been peculiarly under the guidance of God. His directing finger can be seen in every line of its history. By none can this be seen more clearly and by none is it more humbly acknowledged than by those who with solicitude and anxious care have watched its course from the beginning.

But I hear some one say, "You have presented the rosy side of the movement; you have dwelt upon its successes and advances; is there not another side? Have there not been difficulties and setbacks and failures?"

Most assuredly; no such movement as this, so extensive and wide-sweeping, could always expect a plain and easy path. The difficulties that have arisen have largely come from four sources: First, the opposition of denominational authorities, which has resulted in the drawing away of some churches in certain sects* from the inter-denominational movement. But it has gone on with little interruption in its growth, and there seem to be indications in every denomination, with but one exception, of larger fellowship among the young people than in the past. Even in this exceptional denomination the ideas at least of the Christian Endeavor society have been adopted and there seems to be of late in many quarters a distinct swinging back to the interdenominational society —a tendency that is growing every year.

The second cause of partial failure has come from the lack of genuine Christian Endeavor principles. The society has had to suffer for a great many namesakes that were Christian Endeavor societies only in name; societies that had no pledge, little actual service to do for the Master, that put small emphasis upon the committees even if they had any, and that were not embedded in the heart and life of the church as every true society of Christian Endeavor should be. Every organization of every sort, the Christian Church itself not excepted, has to bear the reproach of its own weak and unworthy organizations and members.

* The first denominational societies of the same kind were formed some seven years after the Endeavor movement began.

10   145

Training the Church of the Future

The indifference of some pastors and the coldness of some churches have been from the beginning a source of weakness and an almost insuperable obstacle. The young people of a church can not be expected to rise very much above the spiritual level of the older members. The mercury in their thermometer will stand at about the same degree of temperature as in the thermometer of the older church; or if for a time they have more warmth it is not apt long to withstand the absorbent influence of the neighboring iceberg. When it is declared that the young people's society is a failure total or partial, it is always in order to ask: "Of what sort of a church is it a part and whom does it have for a pastor?" I do not say that the trouble can always be lifted from off its own shoulders, but I do say that I have known very few young people's societies to fail that were guided by warm, loving, sympathetic pastors.

In a recent notable article Mr. Robert Speer, of the Presbyterian Board of Foreign Missions, has written as follows:

"Is there not a risk in our constant emphasis on the truth that the young people should be loyal to the Church, of losing sight of another truth quite as important in my judgment, even more important, namely, the Church's loyalty to the young people? A great deal has been said on the one side, and the young people have not been allowed to lose sight of the duty of loyalty which they owe to their church and their pastor. But

146

loyalty is not a quality to be stated in terms of duty. It is the spontaneous expression of the true and natural devotion of the heart, and no amount of injunction or entreaty will ever produce loyalty in hearts in which it does not spring up as an answer to sympathy and friendliness. No father would think of teaching his little child to love him and be loyal to him by neglecting his child and lecturing it for any lack of a display of affection and fidelity. The father wins the child's love by loving it. He guarantees the child's care for him by caring for the child. It is the father's loyalty to the child that issues in the child's utter loyalty to the father.

"The churches and pastors who have trouble with the loyalty of their young people are usually those who have never set about winning the confidence and fidelity of their young people. It is the genius of young hearts to seek and follow a leader and to worship their heroes. The church that goes to its young people, that cares for them, that gives them worthy service to do, and recognizes their work will never want love and loyalty from its children. There may be exceptions, of course, in local congregations, just as there are in families. A father's loyalty does not inevitably produce a son's loyalty in return. But the only true way of winning the son's loyalty is through the father's love and care."

One other source of weakness is undoubtedly the worldliness of young people. This is a source of weakness common of course to the church and the society of which it is a part. I very much fear that this spirit of worldliness is increasing, and that more difficulties from this source are to be feared in the future than in the past. I scarcely see how it can be otherwise when nominally Christian families, so many more than in years past, patronize and uphold doubtful worldly amusements, train their children by example if not by precept to hold their religion lightly and to seek mammon as well as God. The growing worldliness of a section of the church I think can not be gainsaid, and he who calls attention to it and mourns over it does not deserve the name of pessimist.

Worldly parents will have worldly children. The law of spiritual heredity is more certain than that of physical heredity. It is more certain that religiously indifferent parents will preside over religiously indifferent households than that blue-eyed fathers and mothers will have a blue-eyed flock of children. Where the whole church is indifferent and worldly the young people's society has a hard field indeed. It either gives up the ghost altogether, or lingers on, helpful to and beloved by a fraction of the younger membership, while the "fashionable" people, which is often another name for the worldly, look down with a pitying condescension upon its members as those who are "unco guid" or "righteous overmuch." Yet it is Burns, the author of the former expression, who also says:

> "An Atheist's laugh's a poor exchange
> For Deity offended!"

Other Training Classes

The objections to the society are often urged honestly with a sincere desire that the objections may be removed; sometimes they seem to be offered in a spirit of captiousness and petty fault-finding. Whatever may be their motive, it is not out of place to spend a few moments in considering them.

These objections usually cluster about two points:

First, it is said in many different ways and with many changes rung upon the same theme, that the society divides the church into sections, "chops the church into bits," as some one has graphically expressed it; separates the young from the old, the children from their elders, giving one set of interests to one class and another set to another. Two-thirds of the objections which are urged in print and in private may be traced back to this root. But I would ask, if the real tap-root of this objection does not run much further down than the Young People's Society of Christian Endeavor? Is not this matter that is complained of really a distinction in nature and not in any organization? In fact, when God allowed some people to grow old before others; when He allowed some children to be born in 1850 and others in 1880 and others in 1890, did He not plant all the distinctions that are now observed in the church life of the young and the old and the middle-aged? The same distinctions run through family life and school life. There

149

must be a nursery as well as a parlor and a study in the complete household. There is a primary department, a grammar school, a high school, and a college for those who would have a thorough education. No wise parent insists on living with all the children in one common room for fear that the family will be broken up. No teacher tears down the partitions and merges all the classes into one common schoolroom in order to promote unity of instruction. The great advantage of the modern graded school over the old-fashioned district school where the A–B–C class and the advanced class in algebra all studied in the same room, and where there were often more classes than scholars, is that now the pupils are graded and separated according to their years and ability. Each one gains vastly more than under the old régime. In fact, there is more real unity in the school when thus divided and graded than in the old days.

The family is not divided and split up into fragments because the father goes to his office, the mother to her housework, the children to school or to the ball-ground. It would be absurd and irrational to make this claim. The family all come together at the dinner-table and around the evening fire; they have a thousand opportunities of showing their real unity, and their interest and affection one for another is not weakened but strengthened because sometimes they go their separate ways, only to come together again before the day is over in the common family circle.

Other Training Classes

Nor is the church really divided, when the Juniors have a meeting for an hour once a week by themselves, and the young people have their own weekly hour of prayer and praise and their own activities, and the older people sometimes have meetings for missionary or benevolent purposes that especially appeal to their interests as well. The church family, like the household, separates only to reunite. It has its common interest, its common meeting-places. The Lord's Supper brings all around one common board. The morning service and the evening service of Sunday are alike for all. And in spirit and purpose, in common aims and aspirations and prayers, there is a cord of union which is a thousand times stronger than any mere physical union, at every service of the Lord's house.

In fact the lack of activity on the part of the young in the olden days, their comparative deadness and indifference, were due to the mistaken notion that there could not be different meeting-places and different methods for doing the Lord's work. In many churches the apostle's declaration was forgotten that there were "differences of operations but the same spirit," and as a result young people's societies and meetings were frowned upon, and little Johnny and his older brother and his stalwart father and his wrinkled old grandfather were all treated to the same spiritual pabulum in the weekly meeting—a kind of food which the grandfather relished and usually served, but which did not foster Johnny's growth in grace to any great extent.

If it is true, and it certainly is, that what God hath joined together no man should put asunder, it is equally true that what God hath put asunder through age and natural inclination and adaptability to similar service, no man should join together in an arbitrary and mechanical way.

The most common objection on this score of division, or at least the one that lies at the basis of many others, is the fact that young people are sometimes seen leaving the evening preaching service of Sunday after their own meeting when that meeting comes immediately before this service. This objection, while sometimes valid, is often a superficial and a selfish one. The questions to be considered are not, Do some young people go away? but, Are there not probably more present than there would be were there no young people's meeting? Are the young people as faithful as the older church members? Are there not some reasons which may make absence from the service not only excusable but necessary? Many households have to divide their forces; some going to one service and some to another. Some of the younger ones ought to be at home and a-bed rather than at the later service, and no pastor's heart need burn nor his indignation rise until he finds out whether there are not valid and conscientious reasons why all can not hear his second sermon for the day.

Other Training Classes

After all, fellow students and preachers, there is a good deal of human nature and some remnants of the old Adam left, even in us ministers, we must confess it, and the fact that it is our evening sermon which is not heard rather than the worship of God's house that is not enjoyed, often enters into our disappointment when some one is seen leaving the church. The very fact that it is called commonly the "second service" is an indication of the significance it assumes in many minds. The Sunday-school is in most churches the *second* service; the mission meeting in the outskirts is often the third service; the young people's meeting is not infrequently the fourth service, and the second sermon is the fifth service of the day.

But I am prepared to claim that the young people's movement has *as a rule* increased and strengthened this service, whether it be second, third, fourth, or fifth. On two different occasions I have gathered careful statistics on this point which prove that in proportion to their elders who are also church members the active members of the societies of Christian Endeavor attend the evening preaching service in the proportion of nearly two to one. These are not random or hasty figures, but have been obtained with care from many denominations and from many parts of the country.

The same thing is true in a large measure, tho not quite in such a marked degree, of the mid-week meeting of the church.

In fact, I believe it can be fairly claimed that the young people's movement has promoted the unity of the church. It has shown it its essential oneness. It has led the young people to feel their obligations to the other services of the church as well as to the church services of their own society, for they are all church services. With the gradation has come unity, harmony, and loyalty, for, from the first day of the Christian Endeavor movement, this thought of loyalty, loyalty to the local church, to the denomination and all its work, has been one of the cardinal features of the organization.

The other center of objection to the society of Christian Endeavor has been the character of its meetings, and the prayer-meeting pledge which has largely made them what they are. This is not strange since, as I have before tried to show, the young people's prayer-meeting is a radical departure in many ways from the old prayer-meeting idea. It substituted the thought of practise, training, and the edification that comes from personal participation for the old idea of instruction and edification from the teachings and experience of others. In other words, it substituted the many for the few—the idea of training for the idea of teaching in this particular service.

No wonder that such a departure from tradition should provoke objections. The only answer to such objections, and the amply sufficient one as it seems to me, is, "This plan works well in practise." Is it not an undeniable

Other Training Classes

fact that the young people's meeting of to-day is more
largely attended and more influential, more bright and
interesting, warmer and more spiritual, than ever before?
Has it not introduced into tens of thousands of churches
a new and needed element in training and exercising the
forces of youth? Whatever theoretical objections or
real objections in individual cases there may be, however scrappy or inconsequential, however stumbling or
halting, however perfunctory at times, making all dis-
counts and allowances for not reaching the ideal which
we desire, is it not true that these meetings are, after all,
in nine cases out of ten, perhaps in ninety-nine cases out
of one hundred, centers of genuine spiritual life and
warmth and outreaching activity? Would not all of
these advantages be vastly diminished if these meetings
were given up or essentially changed in their character.
I think the answer, if the pastors and young people
throughout the country alike could be heard from, would
be almost a unanimous and even vociferous, Yes! In
fact, some such questions as these have recently been
asked of the pastors throughout the country; many
thousands have replied, and their answers have been
overwhelmingly in favor of the society and the meeting
which it advocates.

The pledge, being largely responsible for the new departure in the young people's prayer-meeting, has of
course come in for its share of objection and sometimes
objurgation, but I think that it is its letter rather than its

spirit that has been criticized. Every pastor is at liberty to write his own pledge for his own young people. The one commonly used is a suggestion of a possible model rather than a form obligatory upon all. In this matter, as in concerns of more serious moment, the letter killeth, the Spirit giveth life, and the spirit of the Christian Endeavor pledge is that of obligation made so definite and simple that the young heart shall feel the bond and realize the vow. Obligation to take time for personal religious duties, obligation to confess Christ openly and frequently, obligation to be loyal to His church and His service, obligation to bring every duty and every excuse to the touchstone, "What would Jesus have me do?"—surely no Christian who desires the growth of the young in grace and manhood can do anything but rejoice that such obligations are presented, pressed home, and for the most part so willingly accepted and so faithfully performed! These obligations are all in the church covenant, and he who would object to the Christian Endeavor covenant must, in consistency, object to the church covenants of all denominations, which covenants, as a matter of fact, embrace much more than the Christian Endeavor pledge.

And now, in closing these lectures, may I be allowed to urge those who have so patiently and kindly given me their attention to support and carry out as they have opportunity the principles that have been advocated—

adopting and adapting them as circumstances indicate is the will of God?

I am pursued by the fear that I may have seemed to be advocating this Society because of personal pride or glory in an organization. I hope and pray that my purpose is larger and my motive purer. I urge the adoption of these principles and the support of this movement for reasons that I hope will appeal to all of you. At the risk of repetition let me recapitulate them:

In the first place, the Christian Endeavor movement makes for the fellowship and unity of Christians the country over and the world around. It is undoubtedly another tie that binds our hearts in Christian love. The seal of God has been set in a remarkable manner upon this feature of the work. Since He has found a way of promoting loyalty to one's own church and fellowship with those of other folds, can we lightly disregard this road to essential Christian unity which His finger so clearly points out?

If we heard a voice from heaven commanding larger cooperation and unification through such an organization; if we found such a command written in a book which we believed inspired; we should hesitate long before disregarding it. Has not God written His approval of the fellowship born of the Christian Endeavor movement in characters just as unmistakable? Can we disregard or oppose such providential leadings lest haply we be found to fight against God? But the movement in

God's providence is not simply between the denominations of one country, but one that promotes the fellowship of Christians in every land. The unity which God intends has a wider sweep and scope than any of us at first supposed. Young English-speaking Christians have had a link of fellowship forged between them all in America, Great Britain, Australasia, South Africa, such as never has been welded before.

It was an American boy that flew the kite that carried the first cord across the Niagara River which was the means of uniting the two countries, the United States and Canada, with that marvel of engineering skill, the first suspension bridge. In that bridge, in the wire bands of the ocean cable, in the steamships that unite countries which since the world began were separated, we see God's providence in bringing the nations together. Shall we not also recognize His good hand in uniting at the same time with spiritual ties His people for their future conquests? This new century, before its history is told, will need to develop to the utmost every force that can work for righteousness against unrighteousness, for God against greed, for law against lawlessness, for Christ against Beelzebub, and will need to unite all the forces that will range themselves on the side of the King. Here in the Christian Endeavor movement is one of the world's unifiers. Here is one of the ties that bind our hearts in Christian love for Christian service. Can any one then afford to be indifferent to a movement which promises to have a part, if only a modest part, in the lining-up of the righteous forces of the world? Can we afford to let sectarian pride or indifference or prejudice, or some unfortunate experience in local work, prevent us from entering heartily and fully into a work which God seems to indicate may mean so much for the new century?

Again, the indications of Providence seem to show that this movement will make, not only for the fellowship of the churches, but also for democracy in the individual church. Already it has accomplished not a little in this direction. In an unusual way in the young people's meetings the rich and the poor meet together. The simple methods of testimony and prayer, the service that is made possible for the youngest and the most illiterate and backward as well as for the brightest and best educated, tend in a remarkable degree to a democracy which our churches often sorely need to cultivate.

If there is any hateful spirit in the church it is the caste spirit; the Devil is not only the father of lies, but the father of caste distinctions. One of the saddest things that I have seen in this young people's movement is the way in which some members of so-called aristocratic churches hold aloof from it, and in which sometimes the college graduate and the rich and cultured young man will look down upon his brothers and sisters with their simple confession and sometimes ungrammatical testimony.

Training the Church of the Future

Let us sweep all such tawdry travesties of the religion of the meek and lowly Jesus out of our churches. Let us welcome any organization or any movement that will tend to remove from our churches the ancient "gold ring" scandal which is as old as the time of St. James and as low-bred as the Evil One himself.

Sometimes I hear even a minister say, with a slightly patronizing air, that his young people's society does very well for the lower stratum, for the lower middle or the upper middle, according to the snobbish class nomenclature of some people, but that it does not take hold of the educated and the well-to-do—he usually means the fashionable and the worldly; and this is not to be wondered at. But I have yet to find the first earnest Christian, whether rich or poor, educated or uneducated, who can not find help in the sincere, heartfelt testimonies of others, and joy in serving with them. The whole tendency, as I say, is to level these distinctions, to make the gold ring and the fine apparel of less consequence, and to establish and make sure the democracy of Christian believers without which the church will soon lose its grip on average humanity. To promote and increase this spirit, then, I ask for earnest enlistment in our movement, which is one that God is using to this end.

As has been finely said by another, the Society furnishes to the young persons "a ·program of Christianity." Its pledge tells the boy or girl just what it is to be a Christian—trust in Christ, personal devotion,

160

loyalty to His church, confession of love to Him, service for Him.

Once more, it does not savor of boasting, I believe, to say that the society not only promotes the fellowship and the democracy of young disciples, but also their activity in Christian service. These lectures have been of little value if that has not been demonstrated. But I need not rely upon my own impressions or observations. The overwhelming testimony of pastors and active church workers is to the same effect. The crying need of many of our churches is some appropriate Christian work for each of its members. The Society of Christian Endeavor, when properly organized, furnishes just such appropriate service for every one of its members. Many of our non-liturgical churches are constantly losing members to the Episcopal Church, which is being built up in many communities at the expense of the others. One secret of its success is that it quickly furnishes some occupation for all its members from the choir boy to the senior warden. So far forth as it accomplishes this task better than other denominations it deserves its success. The Christian Endeavor Society offers a plan, which has been in successful operation for years, of giving every young man and woman some appropriate and suitable task to accomplish for the Master and His church.

A distinguished author,* in writing of the needs of one denomination of Christians, tho in the same article he is

* President William DeWitt Hyde.

11   161

critical of the Christian Endeavor Society, prescribes five things that the denomination "must do to be saved," as he expresses it. These five things are exactly the things which the society he criticizes stands for. They are as follows;

"1st. It must have a simple and searching covenant." The covenant for active members of the Society of Christian Endeavor is, "Trusting in the Lord Jesus Christ for strength, I promise Him that I will strive to do whatever he would like to have me do." All the duties of the Society are embraced under this head and interpreted by this clause.

"2d. Systematic instruction in what the church stands for." Every prayer-meeting may provide such instruction and stimulus to carry it out, and in this instruction the pastor always has part, and a large part if he will.

"3d. An open door." The door of the Society is wide enough to embrace in some form of membership all the young people of moral earnestness in the community.

"4th. Broad and reasonable requirements of its members." Nothing is required of the members of the Society that Christ would not have them do, and each is left to decide for himself what He requires of them.

"5th. Something definite and practical to do, and personal help in doing it." The exact object of the Christian Endeavor Society could not better be expressed.

That the practical results of this practical training have not been disappointing, is shown by the year-books of those churches that have most cordially adopted the society. In the Presbyterian and Congregational churches and the Disciples of Christ, membership during the past fifteen years has increased far faster than during any preceding fifteen years. More than twice as many have joined these churches on confession of faith each year, on the average, during the last decade and one-half, as in the preceding decade and a half, and the net gain has been twice as great. These figures have recently been obtained by careful investigation and are confirmed by Dr. Daniel Dorchester,* so well known as a careful and conservative statistician.

The auxiliary movements along the line of applied Christianity which have found their way into the Christian Endeavor household and are firmly established there are of much interest as showing the development of Christian life and activity among the young people. None of them has been forced upon the movement, but they have all grown naturally, spontaneously, almost inevitably, from the Christian Endeavor seed. Nor have they proved to be suckers that have robbed the parent plant of its vitality, but each one has brought fresh inspiration and vigor to the movement throughout the world. Chief among these auxiliaries, which have been happily called "the beautiful chapels of the Christian Endeavor cathedral," are "The Quiet Hour," the "Tenth Legion," the "Macedonian Phalanx," the "Home Circle," and the "Civic Club."

Many of these efforts are described by their name

* See article in *Congregationalist*, December, 1900.

and on an earlier page have been alluded to. They can not be dwelt upon at length in this connection, tho some thing more about them will be found in the Appendix.

Am I not justified in appealing to my brother ministers, to those about to enter the ministry, to Sabbath School teachers, and all interested in training the church of the future, to use this method, God-appointed as all its brief history shows, to promote fellowship, democracy, activity, spirituality among the young? He who does not enter into these plans, who holds aloof or withdraws his young people from this brotherhood for sectarian or other reasons, is weakening the fellowship of all, and in a measure detracting from the fellowship, the activity, the inspiration of all. Are there not great and cogent reasons in these days when the common enemy of all righteousness unites his forces against us, for uniting so far as possible our forces against him and for our Lord? Can any one afford to weaken the army of Christian young people because of any small reason, much less a prejudice, which experience might remove? Let me once more repeat that all the plans of the Christian Endeavor movement are flexible, that they may be adapted to any circumstances, that every true society is what its church and pastor desire it to be.

In closing I would record a sentence from a writer to me unknown, which is written in a fly-leaf of the book that contains the original constitution of the original society. It is pregnant with wisdom, and contains the best argument for earnest, faithful, unremitting, systematic effort for Christian nurture:

"Young Christians may make mistakes in working for Christ, but they make a greater mistake in not working for Him. No failure in making the attempt is so bad as to fail to make it. Anything rather than spiritual death. Only let there be vigorous life, and guidance can readily be supplied."

APPENDICES

Appendix I

WORLD-WIDE ENDEAVOR

A BRIEF HISTORY OF THE BEGINNING AND PROGRESS OF THE CHRISTIAN ENDEAVOR SOCIETY IN MANY LANDS.

This brief account of the beginning and spread of the Christian Endeavor Society has been compiled by Mrs. F. E. Clark. The statistics are necessarily incomplete as the numbers are enlarging every year in every land. Yet this chapter will give some idea of the providential spread of the Society.

I.—THE BEGINNING.

Christian Endeavor began in Portland, Me., in 1881. The first society was formed by the Rev. Francis E. Clark, on the second day of February, in the Williston Church. There were about fifty members—boys and girls, as well as young men and women. Their first prayer-meeting was held early in February. The object of the society was to help the boys and girls to be Christians, and to train them to work for Christ. Those boys and girls are now grown up; but most of them are still engaged in Christian work, and we believe that they are doing better service because of their Christian Endeavor training.

II.—GROWTH IN THE UNITED STATES AND CANADA.

In 1882 the first Christian Endeavor Convention was held in Williston Church, Portland. By this time there were about twenty societies in different parts of the country. All of these societies had been formed because these churches had heard of the Christian Endeavor

169

Society in Williston Church and thought it worth trying. The second society was in Newburyport, Mass., the third in Rhode Island, the fourth in Portland, and the fifth in Vermont, and not long after these were formed, societies were heard of in Iowa, New York, New Hampshire, and Canada. As was natural, our nearest neighbor and sister nation, Canada, was the first country outside of the United States to adopt Christian Endeavor.

III.—ENDEAVOR IN HAWAII. (1884.)

A pastor in Honolulu placed in his scrap-book an article by Mr. Clark entitled, "How One Church Takes Care of Its Young People." This article told of Christian Endeavor, and it seemed to this pastor that it would be a good thing for his church; so the first Christian Endeavor Society outside of America was started in Honolulu, and it was a scrap-book article that led to it. These Honolulu Endeavorers often have passing travelers of different nationalities visiting in their meetings, and by them seeds of Christian Endeavor have been carried to many other places. There are now seventeen societies in the Hawaiian Islands.

IV.—CHINA. (1885.)

It was a missionary who carried Christian Endeavor to China. Rev. George H. Hubbard, of Fuchau, a young missionary, took Christian Endeavor with him when he sailed from America. He could not see why it should not be just as good for China, so he organized a society in a church in Fuchau. The first Chinese Endeavorer was Mr. Ling, a very bright young man, who said in an address at a convention in Shanghai that the object of their Christian Endeavor Society was "to drive the devil out of China." They have not wholly succeeded in doing that yet, but the Christian Endeavor Societies all over China are doing something toward it. There is now a United Society for all China, with about two hundred societies enrolled. The first society in Fuchau was called by a Chinese word which means,

170

"The Drum and Rouse Up Society"—not a bad translation of Christian Endeavor. The members of committees had for a badge a small picture-frame wherein were written their instructions, and these frames were passed on to the next committee at the end of six months. It would be a good plan for some of us to try this method used by the first Chinese society.

V.—INDIA, CEYLON, BURMA, SIAM, THE LAOS COUNTRY. (1885——.)

Ceylon.—About the time that Christian Endeavor was starting in China, another missionary, Miss Margaret Leitch, well known in America, was organizing the first society in Ceylon, among some Tamil girls. These girls believed that Christian Endeavor meant, among other things, giving to the Lord, and they set an example to American Endeavorers by consecrating some cocoanut-trees, giving all the cocoanuts that grew on these special trees to missionary work. Was this, perhaps, the beginning of the Tenth Legion?

India.—One of the earliest societies in India was organized in Madanapalle, a mission-station of the Reformed Church of the United States. Soon after societies were formed in many stations connected with the Arcot Mission, and at about the same time others in different parts of India. The second All-India Convention has recently been held in Allahabad, at which missionaries and delegates from all parts of India were present. Dr. Clark has twice visited India; and on the occasion of his last visit, a United Society for India, Burma, and Ceylon, with headquarters at Calcutta, was formed. This United Society has largely promoted the work. Other great unions have been formed, like the South India Union, the Union for the Northwest Provinces, etc. Now there are over four hundred societies in the Madras Presidency of India alone; missionaries of almost all denominations have entered heartily into the work, and Christian Endeavor flourishes in India more than in any other missionary land.

171

Burma, Laos, and Siam.—There are now a few Christian Endeavor Societies in Burma under the care of missionaries, and they are doing what they can to win Burma for Christ. There are twenty-nine societies in the *Laos* country, and two in *Siam*, and their influence is felt in many parts of their countries.

VI.—AFRICA. (1886.)

South Africa.—So far as we know, the first society in Africa was formed in 1886, in Amanzimtote, Natal, and there are now several other societies in these colonies. There is in Durban a native church formed on Christian Endeavor principles. The church members promise to read the Bible every day, or at least to hear it read, for some of them can not read. They also promise to endeavor to give at least one-tenth to the Lord. Tho they have only an occasional visit from a missionary, they are working faithfully. They support twenty-five preaching services every Sunday, some of them going five or six miles to preach. This was in a Zulu church. But the work soon extended to the Dutch and English churches, and soon after was started in Cape Colony and the Boer republics.

When Dr. Clark visited South Africa in 1896, a South African Union was formed at Cape Town, and the societies are multiplying and flourishing finely. This Union has an efficient corps of officers, of which the beloved Andrew Murray is the honorary president. A valuable monthly Christian Endeavor paper is published, and in spite of the long and disastrous war the societies have multiplied throughout South Africa.

Liberia.—The first society in Liberia was organized by Rev. George P. Goll, in the Muhlenberg Mission, in 1891, and soon after several others were formed. The missionaries tell us that these societies have taught their members to be more loyal, liberal, and self-sacrificing, and have bettered their lives in many ways. As the only means of conveyance in Liberia is walking or rowing in a canoe, the loyalty of members who have to travel several miles to attend their meetings can be appreciated. There is now a Liberia Christian Endeavor Union, with seven societies enrolled.

Egypt.—There are several Christian Endeavor Societies in Egypt, in the city of Cairo, and up the Nile, in the mission-churches of the United Presbyterian Church.

Madagascar.—There are ninety-three societies in the island of Madagascar. Tho missionary work has been much hindered in these islands by French occupation, yet a better day is dawning for them, and the missionaries testify that Christian Endeavor is a great help to them in their work.

VII.—GREAT BRITAIN. (1888.)

A young Englishman who had been a member of the first society in Williston Church wrote a letter to his old pastor in England telling him about the society. This pastor became interested in the subject, and as a result of that letter the first English society was started in Crewe, in 1888. At about the same time two or three other pastors, who had in some way heard of it, started societies in their churches. At first there were a good many objections to it in England, and some said that it was a "Yankee notion" which might be good for America, but was not what they needed in England. However, the societies increased, slowly at first and then more rapidly, till there are now (January, 1902) about eight thousand in all Great Britain—and it was a young man's letter to his pastor that began it.

VIII.—AUSTRALASIA. (1888.)

A young man who was a member of the second society of Christian Endeavor, in Newburyport, Mass., sailed on his father's ship from that port to Brisbane, Australia, and told to a pastor there the story of Christian Endeavor, and a society was started in that city.

At about the same time societies were formed in Prahran, a suburb of Melbourne, Victoria, and in one or two other colonies of Australia; for it is a fact that

173

in many countries Christian Endeavor has seemed to blossom out in two or three different places all at once. Wherever a society was formed the young people found it helpful and told their friends about it, and so it came to pass that here and there other societies were formed, until there are now nearly three thousand societies in all the Australian colonies.

In the strength of its Christian Endeavor work, Australia may be considered third of all the countries of the world, ranking after the United States and Canada, which are one in Christian Endeavor, and Great Britain.

The great conventions held in Melbourne, Sydney, Adelaide, and Brisbane are as inspiring as any held in any part of the world. In New Zealand, too, the work flourishes, as well as in Australia, and some of the most ardent Endeavorers to be found in any part of the world are New Zealanders. The Endeavorers of this beautiful island form part of the Australasian Union.

IX.—TURKEY. (1889.)

In 1889 a Christian Endeavor Society was formed in a mission station in Turkey, not far from Cesarea, by an Armenian who had studied in America. The people were at first somewhat prejudiced against it, and called it "one of his American imported ideas." However, he began with his Sunday-school, and presently formed a class of those who were willing to try it. The next year he spoke of it at a conference in Cesare, and the missionaries requested him to prepare a Christian Endeavor Manual in the Turkish language. He found this, however, a work of peculiar difficulty. He says: "I could not safely translate; even the name 'Endeavor' had a military ring in it. 'Society' was forbidden by an imperial edict. Even 'Christian' could not be used, while the term 'Young People' was twice altered. Finally, the title read something like 'Young People's Brotherhood of Moral Activity.' But even this was suppressed by the Turkish censors."

Despite these difficulties, the work has grown and

spread, till there are now scores of societies in Turkey. A missionary writes: "One of the members said to me one day, ' Pastor, we shall beat America.' We may never realize the dream of this young Galatian Endeavorer as to numbers, but in the spirit and degree of consecration it would be difficult to surpass them."

In *Bulgaria* there are several societies of Christian Endeavor, and their members are doing good work "for Christ and the Church."

X.—JAPAN. (About 1889.)

The "Kyoreikwai" is the Japanese name for Christian Endeavor. The first society in Japan was formed by the missionary children of the different stations. Once a year, at the annual meeting of the mission, they hold their meeting all together as a society, and during the rest of the year they meet as branch societies in their separate homes. Sometimes there is a branch society of eight or ten children, as in Kioto, where there are several missionary families, and sometimes only one or two can meet together, as in Okayama, where two little girls held their meeting every week for many years, with their mother for superintendent. These little branch societies tried to be faithful to the pledge, and finally their example was followed by others, and in many places Japanese societies were formed, till there are now seventy-five societies in the Land of the Rising Sun.

XI.—SPAIN. (1889.)

Several years ago, in a mission boarding-school in San Sebastian, a little society was formed among the girls for Christian Endeavor, tho they had not then heard of the societies in America bearing that name. The girls chose the name "Hijas Leales"—Loyal Daughters. They had their meetings, in which all took part, and, as there was very little money in their pockets, they decided to give up some of the food they would otherwise have, and use the money for benevolence. When they heard of Christian Endeavor, and that the societies were branching out into foreign lands, they decided to take that name for the sake of forming part of the great body of Endeavorers. Through the influence of the girls who have gone out from this school other societies have been started in different parts of the country, and there are now thirty-six Christian Endeavor Societies in Spain. There are no more earnest and enthusiastic societies in all the world than those of Spain. Even the Spanish-American war did not interrupt their zeal, tho the society was distinctly identified with America. None of the societies died during that year and several new ones were formed.

XII.—FRANCE. (1889.)

It is through the door of the McAll Mission that Christian Endeavor has entered France. Mr. Greig, who is now at the head of that mission, found that he often came across the words "Christian Endeavor" in religious papers, and he said to a friend, "Something like that is what we need in our work." Later he learned more of the society, and sent for literature on the subject. From the study of the papers that were sent to him grew a little book called "Société d'Activité Chrétienne Status." As information spread, through this little book and in other ways, societies sprang up among the Protestant churches, till there are now sixty-nine societies in France —ten of them in the city of Paris—and tho they pronounce the name a little differently, it means the same thing.

XIII.—PERSIA.

A young lady who was a Christian Endeavorer in America decided at a Christian Endeavor Convention to become a missionary, and not long after went to Hamadan, Persia. She was so enthusiastic for Christian Endeavor that she persuaded Miss Montgomery, who had never seen such a society, to try it there. It was not long before a Junior Endeavor Society was started, which grew out of a prayer-meeting that four little boys had asked for. There are now four Christian Endeavor Societies in Persia, and it is pleasant to remember that it was a Christian Endeavor Convention that started that Christian Endeavor missionary to Persia.

XIV.—MEXICO AND CENTRAL AMERICA. (1891.)

It took just nine years for Christian Endeavor to travel from Maine to Mexico, and the first Christian Endeavor Society in that country was organized in Chihuahua, February 2, 1891. They publish now a Christian Endeavor paper, and there is also a United Society of Christian Endeavor for all Mexico, with three hundred societies enrolled. May the time come when the republic of the South shall rival the republic of the North in Christian Endeavor.

In *Guatemala*, too, Christian Endeavor has made a beginning, and, tho there are only two societies now so far as we know, we hope they may open the door for many more in different parts of Central America.

XV.—SOUTH AMERICA. (1891.)

There are a number of Christian Endeavor Societies in the "Neglected Continent," and tho it goes slowly, as in all Catholic countries, yet wherever Protestant missionaries have gone they have carried Christian Endeavor with them. The first society was formed in Chile, in 1891, and it was greatly helped by some copies of *The Christian Endeavor World* that a New Jersey Endeavor Society sent to them regularly for distribution. These papers have been responsible for much of the Christian Endeavor work done in that country. There are now six societies in Chile, eleven in British Guiana, three in Colombia, and four in Brazil.

XVI.—SWITZERLAND. (1894.)

Three sisters started Christian Endeavor in Switzerland, and the wonder of it is that none of the three had

12   177

ever seen a Christian Endeavor Society. A young
American girl had gone to Lausanne to study French,
and she asked these sisters if there was any Christian
Endeavor Society there. Out of that simple question
has grown the Christian Endeavor work in that country.
Moral: When you are traveling take your Christian
Endeavor with you. There are not yet many societies
in Switzerland, but the number is increasing, and those
who are members are trying in French to keep the same
pledge that we are keeping in English.

XVII.—GERMANY. (1894.)

Through the writings of a German pastor in New
York State news of Christian Endeavor was carried to
Germany. A young theological student became interested in it and tried to interest others, but they had not
much sympathy with it. "Quite good, but American,"
was what they said. It was the story of the Cleveland
Convention that interested a few pastors, and as they
learned more about it, a few societies were formed. At
the first German convention in Berlin one of the speakers
was a young man who had been a member of that first
society in Williston Church, who was then studying
medicine in Berlin. There are now nearly a hundred
societies in Germany, and they call it "Christliche Ent-
schiedenheit." They have a secretary and a monthly
paper of their own. There are also a great many German Christian Endeavor Societies in America, and a
German Christian Endeavor paper, called *Der Mitarbeiter*.

XVIII.—HUNGARY. (1895.)

A young Hungarian who was studying theology in
Berlin was present at the first German Christian Endeavor Convention, and became interested in Christian
Endeavor. He carried the news to Hungary, and a
pastor in a little country church organized a society of
seven members. May this be but the beginning of a
great company of Christian Endeavorers who shall do
what they can to win Hungary for Christ!

178

XIX.—OTHER COUNTRIES IN EUROPE. (1894-99.)

There are in many other countries in Europe small societies here and there. In Sweden there is a great interest in the work, and through the Sunday-School Union thirty-four societies have been formed. The news has lately come of the first society in Russia. Austria has two societies, Belgium two, and Norway four. There are three societies in Italy and two in Denmark. May these few societies in these countries lead the way for many more!

XX.—SYRIA.

The "Nedwat el Ijtehad Messeahy" is what they call it in Syria. If you can not pronounce it you may spell it, but it spells the same thing as Christian Endeavor, tho in a different costume and with different surroundings. There are only a few societies in the Holy Land now, but we hope there will soon be many more of them, and that a Christian Endeavor crusade may some time take even Jerusalem for Christ.

XXI.—THE ISLAND WORLD.

The first Christian Endeavor Society in the South Seas was established at the Malua Training Institute, Upola, Samoa, in 1890. At their first C. E. meeting, ten members were enrolled. Since the establishment of that first society in Samoa two hundred and fifty-eight members have been enrolled in that one society alone. Of these, no less than thirteen have gone as missionaries to New Guinea. We can hardly expect to hear of a South Sea Island Convention, since these islands are scattered over an area of a thousand miles of ocean, but there are now thirteen societies in Samoa alone.

There are also other island societies scattered in different seas and oceans the world around.

The missionaries in the Marshall and Gilbert Islands send most glowing reports of the good the societies are

179

doing in these islands. Probably by this time there are many more societies, as it takes many months to hear reports from them. But according to last advices, there were thirteen societies in the Marshall Islands, two in the Gilbert Islands, six in the Ellice Islands, and three in the Tokelau Islands.

The little island of Jamaica sets a good example to larger islands, for they have there one hundred flourishing Christian Endeavor Societies, and are beginning to talk of a Christian Endeavor Union for all the West Indies.

In Trinidad there are seven societies, and in Granada one.

From the Philippines news comes to us of a society started in the United States Army, the first in those islands. May it be but the forerunner of many more!

And the latest children of Christian Endeavor, so far as we know, are the Cuban societies in Havana, both Young People's and Junior. May those first Endeavorers in that fair island have a large share in the work of winning Cuba for Christ!

XXII.—FLOATING ENDEAVOR.

If any one had predicted when the first society was formed that within less than a dozen years there would be faithful societies sailing the seas, and that they would be found on almost every ocean, he would have been considered a wild prophet, but that is true to-day, and many touching stories have come to us of sailors who are just as faithful to their pledge as any Endeavorers in the home churches. The first Floating Society was formed on the United States Revenue Marine Steamer *Dexter*. Twelve of the sailors signed the pledge, organized a society, and held their first consecration meeting. There are now one hundred and twenty-two societies on board ships of war, and merchant ships, and at life-saving stations. Miss Antoinette P. Jones, by her faithful work, has done much to promote these societies.

Model Constitution

XXIII.—ENDEAVOR IN UNEXPECTED PLACES.

Christian Endeavor has found its way into many unexpected places. In 1890 a society was formed in a Wisconsin State Prison, and the chaplain found it a real help in his work among the prisoners. Because of the good work done in that society, other societies have been organized in other prisons, notably in Kentucky, where a splendid work has been done. Other flourishing prison societies are found in Indiana, Iowa, New Mexico, New York, and several other States. Societies have also been formed in schools, and in hospitals among the nurses, and among policemen, and among traveling men, in the army, and in many other places where no one would have thought of finding them; but their object is always the same, to help their members to be better Christians.

XXIV.—TO-DAY.

To-day (January, 1902) there are fifty-two thousand Christian Endeavor Societies, with nearly three and three-quarter millions of members, in all sorts of places and in almost every country in the world, all pledged to do whatever Jesus would like to have them do.

Appendix II

MODEL CONSTITUTION *

ARTICLE I.—*Name.*

This society shall be called the.....................
YOUNG PEOPLE'S SOCIETY OF CHRISTIAN ENDEAVOR.

* This Constitution, which, in its important features, is substantially the same as that adopted by the first society in Portland, February 2, 1881, has been prepared with great care, and met with the very hearty indorsement of the Fourth National Convention, to which it was presented. It has been revised and approved by the Trustees of the United Society, at a meeting held October, 1887. It is not necessarily binding upon any local society, but is to be regarded in the light of a recommendation, especially for the guidance of new

181

Training the Church of the Future

ARTICLE II.—*Object.*

Its object shall be to promote an earnest Christian life among its members, to increase their mutual acquaintance, and to make them more useful in the service of God.

ARTICLE III.—*Membership.*

1. The members shall consist of three classes: Active, Associate, and Affiliated or Honorary.

2. *Active Members.* The active members of this society shall consist of all young persons who believe themselves to be Christians, and who sincerely desire to accomplish the objects above specified. Voting power shall be vested only in the active members.

3. *Associate Members.* All young persons of worthy character, who are not at present willing to be considered decided Christians, may become associate members of this society. They shall have the special prayers and sympathy of the active members, but shall be excused from taking part in the prayer-meeting. It is expected that all associate members will habitually attend the prayer-meetings, and that they will in time become active members, and the society will work to this end.

4. *Affiliated or Honorary Members.** All persons who,

organizations and those unacquainted with the work of the Society of Christian Endeavor. It is hoped, however, for the sake of uniformity, that the Constitution, which deals only with main principles, may be generally adopted, and that such changes as may be needed to adapt the society to local needs will be made in the By-Laws. Even if the language of the Constitution of some local societies should vary from this Model Constitution, it should be borne in mind that only those societies that adhere to the *prayer-meeting idea* as embodied in Article VII., and the main features of committee work, can properly claim the name of Christian Endeavor societies. The specimen By-Laws which are here appended embrace suggestions for the government of the society which have been found successful in many places. Each one is approved by experience.

* This class of membership is provided for Christians of mature years, especially for those who have been active members, and who desire to remain throughout their lives connected with the society. Young persons who can be either active or associate members should in no case be affiliated members.

182

Model Constitution

tho no longer young, are still interested in the society, and wish to have some connection with it, tho they can not regularly attend the meetings, may become honorary members. Their names shall be kept upon the list under the appropriate heading, but shall not be called at the roll-call meeting. It is understood that the society may look to the honorary members for financial and moral support in all worthy efforts. (For special class of honorary members, see Article XI.)

5. These different persons shall become members, upon being elected by the society, after carefully examining the Constitution and By-Laws and upon signing their names to them, thereby pledging themselves to live up to their requirements.

ARTICLE IV.—*Officers.*

1. The officers of this society shall be a President, Vice-President, Recording Secretary, Corresponding Secretary, and Treasurer, who shall be chosen from among the active members of the society.

2. There shall also be a Lookout Committee, a Prayer-Meeting Committee, a Social Committee, and such other committees as the local needs of each society may require, each consisting of five active members. There shall also be an Executive Committee, as provided in Article VI.

ARTICLE V.—*Duties of Officers.*

1. *President.* The President of the society shall perform the duties usually pertaining to that office. He shall have especial watch over the interests of the society, and it shall be his care to see that the different committees perform the duties devolving upon them. He shall be chairman of the Executive Committee.

2. *Vice-President.* The Vice-President shall assist the President, and perform his duties in his absence.*

3. *Corresponding Secretary.* It shall be the duty of the Corresponding Secretary to keep the local society in

* It is suggested that the Vice-President shall also be Secretary of the Executive Committee.

183

communication with the State and local Christian Endeavor unions and with the United Society, and to present to his own society such matters of interest as may come from the United Society, from other local societies, and from other authorized sources of Christian Endeavor information. This office shall be held permanently by the same person, so long as he is able to perform its duties satisfactorily, and his name should be forwarded to the United Society immediately after election.

4. *Recording Secretary.* It shall be the duty of the Recording Secretary to keep a record of the members, to correct it from time to time, as may be necessary, and to obtain the signature of each newly elected member to the Constitution; also to correspond with absent members, and to inform them of their standing in the society; also to keep correct minutes of all business meetings of the society; also to notify all persons elected to office or to committees.

5. *Treasurer.* It shall be the duty of the Treasurer to keep safely all moneys belonging to the society, and to pay out only such sums as shall be voted by the society.

ARTICLE VI.—*Duties of Committees.*

1. *Lookout Committee.* It shall be the duty of this committee to bring new members into the society, to introduce them to the work and to the other members, and affectionately to look after and reclaim any that seem indifferent to their duties, as outlined in the pledge. This committee shall also, by personal investigation, satisfy itself of the fitness of young persons to become members of this society, and shall propose their names at least one week before their election to membership, having first presented such names to the pastor for approval.

2. *Prayer-Meeting Committee.* It shall be the duty of this committee to have in charge the prayer-meeting, and to see that a topic is assigned and a leader appointed for every meeting, and to do what it can to secure faithfulness to the prayer-meeting pledge.

3. *Social Committee.* It shall be the duty of this com-

Model Constitution

mittee to promote the social interests of the society by welcoming strangers to the meetings, and by providing for the mutual acquaintance of the members by occasional sociables, for which any appropriate entertainment, of which the church approves, may be provided.

4. *Executive Committee.** This committee shall consist of the pastor of the church, the officers of the society, and the chairmen of the various committees. All matters of business requiring debate shall be brought first before this committee, and by it reported to the society either favorably or adversely. All discussions of proposed measures shall take place before this committee, and not before the society. Recommendations concerning the finances of the society shall also originate with this committee.

5. Each committee, except the Executive, shall make a report in writing to the society, at the monthly business meetings, concerning the work of the past month.

ARTICLE VII.—*The Prayer-Meeting.*

All the active members shall be present at every meeting, unless detained by some absolute necessity, and each active member shall take some part, however slight, in every meeting. To the above all the active members shall pledge themselves, understanding by "absolute necessity" some reason for absence which can conscientiously be given to their Master, Jesus Christ.

ARTICLE VIII.—*The Pledge.*†

All persons on becoming active members of the Society shall sign the following pledge:

Trusting in the Lord Jesus Christ for strength, I promise Him that I will strive to do whatever He would like to have me do; that I will make it the rule of my life to pray and to

* The object of this committee is to prevent waste of time in the regular meetings of the society by useless debate and unnecessary parliamentary practise, which are always harmful to the spirit of a prayer-meeting.

† If this exact form of words is now adopted, it is earnestly hoped that it will not be essentially weakened, but that a pledge em-

185

read the Bible every day, and to support my own church in every way, especially by attending her regular Sunday and mid-week services, unless prevented by some reason which I can conscientiously give to my Savior; and that, just so far as I know how, throughout my whole life, I will endeavor to lead a Christian life

As an active member, I promise to be true to all my duties, to be present at, and to take some part, aside from singing, in every Christian Endeavor prayer-meeting, unless hindered by some reason which I can conscientiously give to my Lord and Master. If obliged to be absent from the monthly consecration meeting of the society, I will, if possible, send at least a verse of Scripture to be read in response to my name at the roll call.

Signed....................   ....

The associate member's pledge is as follows:

ASSOCIATE MEMBER'S PLEDGE.

As an associate member, I promise to attend the prayer meetings of the society habitually, and declare my willing-ness to do what I may be called upon to do as an associate member to advance the interests of the society

Signed.................... ....

ARTICLE IX.—*The Consecration Meeting.*

1. Once each month a consecration or covenant meet-ing shall be held, at which each active member shall re-new his vows of consecration. If any one chooses, he can express his feelings by an appropriate verse of Scrip-ture or other quotation.

2. At each consecration meeting the roll shall be called (or some equally thorough method of making the record may be adopted), and the responses of the active mem-bers shall be considered as renewed expressions of alle-giance to Christ. *It is expected that if any one is obliged to be absent from this meeting, he will send a message, or at*

bracing the ideas of private devotion, loyalty to the church, and outspoken confession of Christ in the weekly meeting will be adopted. When the Prayer-Meeting Pledge is carefully studied it will be seen that only the common duties of the Christian life are demanded, private prayer and Bible study, outspoken confession of Christ before men, and loyalty to Christ's church. All this is em-bodied in every church covenant. It is here made specific and definite for immature and inexperienced Christians.

Model Constitution

least a verse of Scripture, to be read in response to his name at the roll-call.

3. If any active member of this society is absent from this monthly meeting, and fails to send a message, the Lookout Committee is expected to take the name of such a one, and in a kind and brotherly spirit ascertain the reason for the absence. *If any active member of the society is absent and unexcused from three consecutive monthly meetings, such a one ceases to be a member of the society, and his name, on vote of the Lookout Committee and the pastor, shall be stricken from the list of members.*

4. Any associate member who, without good reason, is regularly absent from the prayer-meetings, and shows no interest whatever in the work of the society, may, upon vote of the Lookout Committee and pastor, be dropped from the roll of members.

ARTICLE X.—*Business Meetings and Elections.*

1. Business meetings may be held in connection with the prayer-meeting, or at any other time in accordance with the call of the President.

2. An election of the officers and committees shall be held once in six months.* Names may be proposed by a Nominating Committee appointed by the President, of which the pastor shall be a member *ex officio*.

ARTICLE XI.—*Relation to the Church.*

This society, being a part of the church, owes allegiance only and altogether to the church with which it is connected. The pastors, deacons, elders or stewards, and Sunday-school superintendent, if not active members, shall be, *ex officiis*, honorary members. Any difficult question shall be laid before them for advice, and their decision shall be final. It shall be understood that the nomination of officers or other action taken by the society shall be subject to revision or veto by the church; that in every way the society shall put itself under the

* Once a year, if preferred.

187

control of the official board of the church, and shall make a report to the church monthly, quarterly, or annually, as the church may direct.

ARTICLE XII.—*Relation of the Junior Society.*

The Young People's Society of Christian Endeavor and the Junior Society being united by ties of closest sympathy and common effort, monthly (or at least annual) reports should be read to the Young People's Society by the Junior Superintendent. When the boys and girls reach the age of fourteen, they shall be transferred to the older society. Special pains shall be taken to see that a share of the duties and responsibilities of the prayer-meetings and of the general work of the society shall be borne by the younger members.

ARTICLE XIII.—*Fellowship.*

This society, while owing allegiance only to its own church, is united by ties of spiritual fellowship with other Christian Endeavor societies the world around. This fellowship is based upon a common love of Christ, is cemented by a common pledge and common methods of work, and is guaranteed by a common name, "Christian Endeavor," used either alone or in connection with some denominational name.

This fellowship is that of an interdenominational, not an undenominational, organization. It is promoted by local-union meetings, State and national conventions, and still further by the work of the Information Committee, which it is hoped will be adopted by each society. (See By-Laws, Article X.)

ARTICLE XIV.—*Withdrawals.*

Any member who may wish to withdraw from the society shall state the reasons to the Lookout Committee and pastor, and if these reasons seem sufficient he may be allowed to withdraw.

188

Model Constitution

ARTICLE XV.—*Miscellaneous.*

Any other committees may be added and duties assumed by this society which in the future may seem best.

ARTICLE XVI.—*Transfer of Members.*

Since it would in the end defeat the very object of our organization if the older active members, who have been trained in the society for usefulness in the church, should remain content with fulfilling their pledge to the society only, therefore it is expected that the older members, when it shall become impossible for them to attend two weekly prayer-meetings, shall be transferred to the honorary membership of the society, if previously faithful to their vows as active members. This transfer, however, shall be made with the understanding that the obligation to faithful service shall still be binding upon them in the regular church prayer-meeting. It shall be left to the Lookout Committee, in conjunction with the pastor, to see that this transfer of membership is made as occasion requires.

ARTICLE XVII.—*Amendment.*

This Constitution may be amended at any regular business meeting, by a two-thirds vote of the entire active membership of the society, provided that a written statement of the proposed amendment shall have been read to the society and deposited with the Secretary at the regular business meeting next preceding.

SPECIMEN BY-LAWS.*

ARTICLE I.

This society shall hold a prayer-meeting on.........evening of each week. The.........regular prayer-meeting of the month shall be a consecration meeting, at which the roll shall be called.

* If it is thought that these rules and regulations are unnecessarily long, it should be borne distinctly in mind that these specimen By-Laws are simply given as *suggestions*

Article II.—*Method of Conducting the Consecration Meeting.*

At this meeting the roll may be called by the leader during the meeting or at its close. After the opening exercises, the names of five or more may be called, and then a hymn sung or a prayer offered. The committees may be called by themselves, or other variations of the roll-call introduced. Thus varied, with singing and prayer interspersed, the entire roll shall be called.

Article III.—*Business Meetings.*

The society shall hold its regular business* meeting in connection with the.........regular prayer-meeting in the month. Special business meetings may be held at the call of the President.

Article IV.—*Elections.*

The election of officers and committees shall be held at the first business meeting in........................

A Nominating Committee shall be appointed by the President at least two weeks previous to the time for electing new officers. Of this committee the pastor shall be a member *ex officio.* It is understood that these officers are chosen subject to the approval of the church. If there is no objection on the part of the church, the election stands. The following causes of the By-Laws may be read at the society before each semi-annual election of officers:

While membership on the board of officers or committees of this society should be distributed as evenly as the best good of the society will warrant, among the different members, the offices shall not be considered places of honor to be striven for, but simply opportunities for

---

* This business meeting will usually be simply for the hearing of reports from the committees, or for such matters as will not detract from the spiritual tone of the meeting. All matters requiring discussion, it will be remembered, are to be brought before the Executive Committee, and not before the society.

increased usefulness, and any ill feeling or jealousy springing from this cause shall be deemed unworthy a member of the Society of Christian Endeavor. When, however, a member has been fairly elected, it is expected that he will consider his office a sacred trust, to be conscientiously accepted, and never to be declined except for most urgent and valid reasons.

ARTICLE V. — *New Members.**

Applications for membership may be made on printed forms, which shall be supplied by the Lookout Committee and returned to them for consideration.

Names may be proposed for membership one week before the business meeting, and shall be voted on by the society at that meeting. The Lookout Committee may, in order to satisfy itself of the Christian character of the candidate, present to all candidates for active or associate membership the, appropriate membership pledge to be signed. (The form of these pledges may be found elsewhere.)

ARTICLE VI.

Persons who have forfeited their membership may be readmitted on recommendation of the Lookout Committee and pastor and by vote of the members present at any regular business meeting.

ARTICLE VII.

New members shall sign the Constitution, which shall contain the pledge, within four weeks from their election, to confirm the vote of the society.

---

* Great care should be taken that new members understand their duties and the obligations of the pledge. and it should be explained to them how reasonable, Scriptural, and possible of fulfilment it is. Emphasis should be laid upon the fact that nothing more is demanded in the Christian Endeavor pledge than in the average church covenant. only the duties are made specific; also that an excuse which one can give to the Master is always accepted, and that no other should be urged for the non-performance of any duty.

ARTICLE VIII.

Any one who can not accept the office to which he may be elected shall notify the President before the next business meeting, at which the vacancy shall be filled. In the mean time, the former officer holds the position.

ARTICLE IX.

Letters of introduction to other Christian Endeavor societies shall be given to members *in good standing* who apply to be released from their obligations to the society, this release to take effect when they shall become members of another society; until then, their names shall be kept on the Absent List. Members removing to other places, or desiring to join other Christian Endeavor societies in the same city or town, are requested to obtain letters of introduction within six months from the time of their leaving, unless they shall give satisfactory reasons to the society for their further delay.

ARTICLE X.

Other committees may be added, according to the needs of local societies, whose duties may be defined as follows:

Information Committee. It shall be the duty of this committee to gather information concerning Endeavorers or Endeavor work in all parts of the world, and to report the same. For this purpose, five minutes shall be set aside at the beginning of each meeting.

Sunday-School Committee. It shall be the duty of this committee to endeavor to bring into the Sunday-school those who do not attend elsewhere, and to cooperate with the Superintendent and officers of the school in any ways which they may suggest for the benefit of the Sunday-school.

Calling Committee. It shall be the duty of this committee to have a special care for those among the young people who do not feel at home in the church, to call on them, and to remind others where calls should be made.

Music Committee. It shall be the duty of this committee to provide for the singing at the young people's meeting, and also to turn the musical ability of the society to account, when necessary, at public religious meetings.

Missionary Committee. It shall be the duty of this committee to provide for regular missionary meetings, to interest the members of the society in all ways in missionary topics, and to aid, in any manner which may seem practicable, the cause of home and foreign missions.

Flower Committee. It shall be the duty of this committee to provide flowers for the pulpit, and to distribute them to the sick at the close of the Sabbath services.

Temperance Committee. It shall be the duty of this committee to do what may be deemed best to promote temperance principles and sentiment among the members of the society.

Relief Committee. It shall be the duty of this committee to do what it can to cheer and aid, by material comforts if possible and necessary, the sick and destitute among the young people of the church and Sunday-school.

Good-Literature Committee. It shall be the duty of this committee to do its utmost to promote the reading of good books and papers. To this end it shall do what it can to circulate the religious newspaper representing the society among its members, also to obtain subscribers for the denominational papers or magazines among the families of the congregation as the pastor and church may direct. It may, if deemed best, distribute tracts and religious leaflets, and in any other suitable way which may be desired introduce good reading matter wherever practicable.

Other committees not here found may be added as occasion may demand and the church may desire.

ARTICLE XI.

Members who can not meet with this society for a time are requested to obtain leave of absence, which shall be granted by the Lookout Committee and pastor and withdrawn at any time by the same, and their names shall be placed on the Absent List.

ARTICLE XII.

.... .members shall constitute a quorum.

ARTICLE XIII.

These By-Laws may be amended by a two-thirds vote of the members present at any regular meeting, provided that notice of such amendment is given in writing and is recorded by the Secretary at least one week before the amendment is acted upon.

Appendix III

JUNIOR SOCIETIES OF CHRISTIAN ENDEAVOR

The demand for Junior societies has been as spontaneous as it is pressing. It is a natural and inevitable outgrowth of the Christian Endeavor movement. Many pastors and churches have felt that, while the Young People's Society of Christian Endeavor was admirably answering the needs of the young men and women, and of the older boys and girls, yet the younger boys and girls, who could not attend the regular weekly prayer-meeting held in the evening, were, in some degree, left out of the plan. In thousands of churches this lack has been supplied by the introduction of Junior Societies of Christian Endeavor, into which the children are taken, and from which they are graduated, when old enough, into the Young People's Society. The suggestions here given have come to me very largely from others who have successfully tried these plans.

WHO SHOULD BELONG?

Various answers are given to this question. The practise of wise superintendents differs in regard to the age limit, tho the usual age is, perhaps, from seven to fourteen. A child might attend and be a preparatory member as soon as he is old enough to understand that he must be quiet and reverent during the meeting. Still, it is difficult to draw any age limit on the younger side, and perhaps it is not necessary. The age line is drawn largely by the necessities of the case.

The call for Junior societies comes from the fact that there are many boys and girls who ought to be brought under direct religious influence whose parents will not, and should not, allow them to go out in the evening, when meetings of the Young People's Society are necessarily held. For them meetings should be appointed in the afternoon (and a week day is better than Sunday), or at least in the early evening. It is also true that these younger children, while there are many things in their society which they can do for themselves, are not quite old enough to carry on their organization fully. They particularly need the guidance of some older Christian friends. This brings us to the question:

WHO SHOULD BE AT THE HEAD OF THE JUNIOR SOCIETY?

Some one or two or more of the older and more judicious members of the Young People's Society, I should say; but be sure they have a great love for children in their hearts. They will need tact and "consecrated common sense."

WHAT PLEDGE SHOULD THE CHILDREN TAKE?

A pledge as much like the pledge of the older society as their years will allow. I do not think it is too much to ask of even the boys and girls of seven or eight to pray and read the Bible every day, to try and live Christian lives, and to show it by being present at the weekly meeting and taking some part therein. There are some expressions of the Christian life which are just as appropriate to the boy of eight as to the youth of eighteen or the man of forty-eight, and it is just as important that he should give utterance to these expressions.

We do not expect a little oration or a vivid experience each week from them. The Christian Endeavor idea is utterly antagonistic to anything of that sort; but there are simple words of confession which are just as appropriate for the little child to use as the more elaborate forms are for his father.

There is no danger of beginning too young. Our older societies will be stronger, and so will our churches, if these little ones begin aright. In churches where there are flourishing Junior as well as Young People's Societies of Christian Endeavor, I predict very few "dumb Christians" in twenty years from now. One of the dangers that will meet the superintendent is that of trying to do all the work and most of the talking. A Junior society is not a primary Sunday-school class. It is a training-school where the children learn by speaking and praying and filling the offices and working on the committees.

And now for the conclusion of the whole matter: If, in your Sunday-school, there are a number of boys and girls who are too young for the regular society, but not too young to come to Jesus and be trained for Him, consider carefully whether the Junior society is not the thing for them. Count the cost; remember that it will require work for some one to keep it in a flourishing condition. (The difficulty is not in starting, but in sustaining such a society.) Then if you are convinced that such an auxiliary is what you need, go forward and start a Junior society "for Christ and the Church."

MODEL CONSTITUTION AND BY-LAWS.

ARTICLE I.—*Name.*

This society shall be called the JUNIOR SOCIETY OF CHRISTIAN ENDEAVOR OF ....
....

Junior Societies

ARTICLE II.—*Object.*

Its object shall be to promote an earnest Christian life among the boys and girls who shall become members, and prepare them for the active service of Christ.

ARTICLE III.—*Membership.*

1. The members shall consist of two classes, active and preparatory.*

2. *Active members.* Any boy and girl between the ages of..........and.........., inclusive, who shall be approved by the superintendent and assistant, may become an active member of the society by taking the following pledge:

JUNIOR MEMBERSHIP PLEDGE.

Trusting in the Lord Jesus Christ for strength, I promise Him that I will strive to do whatever He would like to have me do, that I will pray and read the Bible every day, and that, just so far as I know how, I will try to lead a Christian life. I will be present at every meeting of the society when I can, and will take some part in every meeting.

Name..................................

I am willing that..... ....should sign this pledge, and will do all I can to help..........keep it

Parent's name......... ....

Residence... ... .

3. *Preparatory members* shall be those who wish to belong to the society, but whose parents are not quite ready to let them sign the pledge. They will be expected to attend the meetings regularly, and it is hoped that this will be considered simply as a preparation for active membership.

* NOTE.—Some societies also provide for Honorary members, consisting of the pastor, President of the Young People's Society, and mothers that are especially interested in the society and desire to help it by their prayers and occasional attendance.

197

The preparatory members shall take the following pledge:

> As a preparatory member I promise to be present at every meeting when I can, and to be quiet and reverent during the meeting.
> Signed.................................

ARTICLE IV.—*Officers.*

The officers of the society shall be one or more superintendents chosen by the Young People's Society, with the approval of the church and pastor; also a President, Vice-President, Secretary, and Treasurer, who shall be chosen by the boys and girls. There shall also be a Lookout Committee, a Prayer-Meeting Committee, a Social Committee, a Missionary Committee, and such other committees as the superintendents may deem best. These committees shall be nominated by the superintendents and elected by the society.

ARTICLE V.—*Duties of Officers.*

1. The *Superintendent* shall have full control of the society.

2. The *Assistant Superintendent* shall aid the Superintendent in her work. The Assistant shall take care of all funds belonging to the society, the money being turned over to her by the Treasurer at the close of each meeting.

3. The *President* shall conduct the business meetings, under the direction of the Superintendent.

4. The *Vice-President* shall act in the absence of the President.

5. The *Secretary* shall keep a correct list of the members, take the minutes of the business meetings, and call the names at the roll-call meetings.

6. The *Treasurer* shall take up the collections, enter the amount in the account-book, and turn over the money to the Assistant Superintendent, and also enter all expenditures as directed by the Superintendent.

Junior Societies

ARTICLE VI.—*Duties of Committees.*

1. The *Lookout Committee* shall secure the names of any who may wish to join the society, and report the same to the superintendents for action. They shall also obtain excuses from members absent from the roll-call, and affectionately look after and reclaim any who seem indifferent to their pledge.

2. The *Prayer-Meeting Committee* shall, in connection with the Superintendent, select topics, assign leaders, and do what it can to secure faithfulness to the prayer-meeting pledge.

3. The *Social Committee* shall welcome the children to the meetings, and introduce them to the other members of the society. They may also arrange for occasional sociables.

ARTICLE VII.—*Relationship.*

The Junior society is a part of the church, and its relation to the Young People's Society of Christian Endeavor should be close and intimate. It is expected that when the members of the Junior society have reached their age limit, they will enter the Christian Endeavor Society as active members.

ARTICLE VIII.—*Meetings.*

1. A prayer-meeting shall be held once every week. A consecration meeting shall be held once a month, at which the pledge shall be read and the roll called, and the responses of the members shall be considered a renewal of the pledge of the society. If any member is absent from three consecutive consecration meetings, without excuse, his name shall be dropped from the list of members.

2. Part of the hour of the weekly meeting may, if deemed best, be used by the pastor or Superintendent of the society for instruction, or for other exercises which they may approve.

BY-LAWS.*

1. The society shall hold a prayer-meeting on........
................of each week. The last regular
meeting of each month shall be a consecration meeting.
The business meeting may be held in connection with the
first regular meeting of each month.

2. The officers and committees shall be chosen in
..........and.... .....and continue six months, beginning on the first of the month following their election.

3. Special meetings of the society may be held at any
time, at the call of the Superintendent.

4. A collection shall be taken at the consecration meeting, and at the other meetings if desired, the money thus
obtained to be held available for benevolent objects and
to meet the expenses of the society.

5. All committees should meet at least once a month
for consultation with the Superintendent in regard to
their work.

6. All expenditures shall be made under the direction
of the Superintendent.

7. Other committees may be added, whose duties shall
be defined as follows:

The *Music Committee* shall distribute and collect the
singing-books, and cooperate with the leader of the
meeting in trying in every way to make the singing a
success.

The *Missionary Committee* shall arrange for an occasional
missionary meeting, and seek to interest the members in
home and foreign work.

The *Temperance Committee* shall arrange for an occasional temperance meeting, and circulate a temperance
pledge among the members.

The *Sunday-School Committee* shall secure the names of
children who do not attend Sunday-school, and invite
them to become members of the Sunday-school.

* It is hoped that so far as possible the societies will adhere to the
Model Constitution, making all necessary local changes in the By-
laws.

The *Flower Committee* shall provide flowers for the Sunday-school room, and distribute fruit and flowers to the sick and needy.

The *Scrap-Book Committee* shall collect pictures and clippings, and make scrap-books for sick and disabled members and for distribution in the hospitals.

The *Relief Committee* shall collect clothing for the destitute children found in the Sunday-school and society, and bring it to the Superintendent for distribution.

The *Birthday Committee* shall report all birthdays as they occur among the members, so that special prayer may be offered for each member on his or her birthday.

8. This Constitution and these By-Laws may be altered or amended any time the superintendents and pastor find it necessary.

Appendix IV

CHRISTIAN ENDEAVOR AS A WORLD-WIDE MOVEMENT, AND ITS CLAIM UPON THE CHURCHES

By FRANCIS E. CLARK, D.D.

Occasionally I hear of a pastor who gives up his Christian Endeavor society as an old coat would be laid aside, or of a church that disbands its society as jauntily as a housewife discharges her cook.

Ten times oftener I hear of new societies being formed and of pastors and churches guarding them as choice treasures. Still, the former cases occur often enough to call for a few words of comment, and to lead me to ask and to attempt to answer the question, What claim has Christian Endeavor as a movement upon the churches?

FIRST.

It has a claim because it stands for the largest and strongest Christian fellowship and federation of Christian young people known to-day. A society that drops out of the ranks of Christian Endeavor drops out of this fellowship, and there is nothing to take its place.

There is absolutely no other interdenominational and international Christian federation in the world for young people, and nothing like it as yet for the older people of our churches.

While we have been longing for the spiritual federation, and praying for it, and singing about it, it has come without observation, and is an actual fact.*

Second.

Christian Endeavor can and does promote an *esprit de corps* that is possible only because the movement is so widespread in the nations and denominations.

The Standard Dictionary defines the above French phrase as a "spirit of common devotedness, sympathy, or support among the members of an association or body"; and this is a most valuable asset of Christian Endeavor.

It increases the value of every society to its own church. It affects for good every prayer-meeting. It may inspire every committee. It thrills every convention.

Moreover, this and the other wider aspects and results of Christian Endeavor are so plainly *providential* that they can not wisely be neglected by any thinking Chris-

---

*The impression is sometimes industriously circulated that as a federation of the young people of the churches, Christian Endeavor has failed, and that a new federation is needed. Let us see what denominations are in the Christian Endeavor federation already. Practically all the Presbyterians, Congregationalists, Disciples of Christ, Christians, Moravians, Cumberland Presbyterians, Reformed Presbyterians, Reformed Church of America, and the Reformed Church in the United States, the United Evangelical Association, Reformed Episcopal, Methodist Protestant, Primitive Methodist, Free Baptists, Mennonites, Church of God, Friends, African Methodist Episcopal, and African Methodist Episcopal Zion, large sections of the Baptist, Lutheran, United Presbyterian, and United Brethren churches, and smaller sections of the Protestant Episcopal and Methodist Episcopal churches. This in the United States alone; while in Canada and other countries our fellowship is even more inclusive. Surely this is a goodly federation to have grown up virtually in twenty years!

tian. They have not been built up with pains and toil by any man. They have all grown from a seed of God's planting. Is it not fair to say that he who opposes them seems to oppose one of God's methods of training and inspiring the young?

THIRD.

Christian Endeavor stands peculiarly for Christian citizenship.

As a movement it can do for this great cause, so dear to every patriot, what is utterly impossible for a local society or a purely denominational organization that has no affiliations with a world-movement. It can propose and project efforts, and bring things to pass, and hold inspiring mass-meetings that are impossible except where millions of youth in many communions are banded together. For instance, the memorial in behalf of peace and international arbitration, which received the distinguished approval of The Hague Peace Commissioners, and the "Civic Clubs," recently proposed for the discussion and study of municipal affairs, are two examples from many of what is possible only to a general movement and impossible to a local society.

FOURTH.

Christian Endeavor stands for Christian missions, and can do so in the most effective way because it exists in a hundred denominations and in fifty countries. The sense of brotherhood with a multitude of other young Endeavorers of every nation and kindred and people and tongue beneath the sun, is necessary to the full quickening of missionary zeal of the largest, most catholic, and most Christ-like quality. The local society that withdraws from this fellowship must inevitably lose something of this quickening sense of enthusiasm for the redemption of the world.

FIFTH.

Christian Endeavor has lately come to stand for the Christian home, and will increasingly be identified with this thought. "Family Worship," "Household Religion," "Filial Piety," will be written upon its banners. These are great words and greatly needed efforts, which can be projected and promoted only by a national and international movement.

It is not likely to be shared in fully except by the societies that are in the movement.

SIXTH.

Christian Endeavor stands for the Quiet Hour of meditation and communion with God. It advocates it, furnishes helps for it, identifies itself with this thought in all its publications and conventions. Such an effort to embody and vivify in millions of hearts a great truth like this is possible only to a movement that is found in every church and every land.

SEVENTH.

The experiment of independence is not an untried one. First and last, during the last twenty years, the plan has been tried many times of withdrawing from the Christian Endeavor fellowship and setting up an independent society, or a purely denominational society.

Has there been any corresponding gain to compensate for the heavy losses? Are the prayer-meetings of the independent societies more helpful; is their committee work more efficient; is their loyalty more unquestioned? I have never heard that this was the case in a single instance. I have often heard of irreparable losses in these respects.

EIGHTH.

Here is a movement that has grown up from a tiny mustard-seed in the providence of God.

It has not been built with ecclesiastical hammer and nails, or stuck together with the adhesive plaster of churchly authority. It has a natural, spontaneous, necessary growth from the seed.

The seed flourishes in any garden-spot the world around where it is cared for. If it is not growing straight and comely, it can be pruned and invigorated and trained. It can always be mended; it need never be ended.

The church that gives up its society of Christian Endeavor is giving up not a name, not a method, not a form of pledge merely. In all these things the Society is flexible, and may be adapted to any church or denomination.

NINTH.

It is not simply giving up connection with a United Society or World's Union, but it is giving up a world-wide fellowship and its share in helping and being helped by tens of thousands of other societies and nearly four millions of other young people, to be more useful in other churches, to be better citizens, better missionaries to others, better home-makers, better men and women.

Are these things to be lightly treated and carelessly put one side?

Not a few societies that have isolated themselves from the movement, or have been withdrawn from it by pastor or church, have come back into it with new appreciation of its value. In the name of the Christian Endeavor hosts the world around, we cordially and heartily invite all young people's societies of similar aims and methods to join the ever-increasing ranks of Christian Endeavor, that we may have the blessing of their fellowship, and that they may share the inspiration, the fellowship, the zeal, the tried and prove methods of a world-movement.

Appendix V

A QUIET-HOUR CATECHISM

By FRANCIS E CLARK, D.D.

The following questions and answers will perhaps help some to a better understanding of the Quiet Hour.

Question.—What is the Quiet Hour?

Answer.—It is the time set apart each day for personal communion with God.

Ques.—Why should we keep the Quiet Hour?

Ans.—Because our souls need it. Because our work demands it, and the larger our work and the busier our lives, the more we need it. Because otherwise God is likely to get crowded out of our busy lives. Because Christ's example commends it. Because every eminent saint has practised such quiet communion. Because we should take time to talk with God, as well as for business, school, or pleasure. Because we must listen to God before we can do His will. Because it will give a new meaning to prayer, and make of the Bible a different book to us. Because all who have practised it faithfully tell us it has brought joy and sweetness into their lives, and power for service. Because they all unite in saying that when faithfully observed it makes life infinitely fuller and richer.

Ques.—How should the Quiet Hour be kept?

Ans.—Each one must decide for himself. Part of it will be spent in reading, with meditation, devotional passages of the Bible; part, perhaps, in reading some devotional book; part in petition for special blessing; but some part should also be spent in sitting quietly before God, realizing, "practising" His presence; opening the soul to Him; listening to His voice.

Ques.—Is there not danger that it will cultivate a morbid introspectiveness, or separate life into sacred and secular periods?

Ans.—This is not the experience of those who have practised it. It has made *all* of life more wholesome and better worth living, and has brought the presence of God into every humble daily task.

Ques.—Does the "Quiet Hour" mean a literal hour of sixty minutes?

Ans.—No, it means "at least fifteen minutes," better still, half an hour; enough time genuinely to realize the presence of God, and quietly to commune with Him.

A Quiet-Hour Catechism

We believe that fifteen minutes a day is the least time that should thus be given.

Ques.—Must the Quiet Hour always be observed in the morning?

Ans.—No, the title "Quiet Hour" was deliberately chosen rather than the "Morning Watch" to give liberty in the time of its observance; but we very strongly advise the first morning hour immediately on rising and before breakfast. Busy men and women will find this almost the only time of which they can be sure.

Ques.—Can others besides Endeavorers become "Comrades of the Quiet Hour"?

Ans.—Yes. Any one who will, young or old. We hope Endeavorers will get as many other Christians as possible to join them as "Comrades."

Ques.—Can one ever withdraw from membership?

Ans.—Yes, at any time, by sending word and asking to have the name taken from the list of the Comrades.

Ques.—But supposing I should forget, or over-sleep, or be taken delirious, or for some reason I should fail to keep the Quiet Hour, should I not be perjuring myself if I sign this covenant?

Ans.—No, because we promise to make it "the rule of our life," and a "rule" allows reasonable and necessary exceptions. But when we once learn the blessedness of the Quiet Hour, we shall find that there will be very few exceptions to the rule.

Ques.—Will subjects be given for meditation, and directions for making the most of the Quiet Hour?

Ans.—Yes; suggestions of this sort will be made, which can be followed or not as each one pleases. *The Christian Endeavor World* will take special pains to give many hints and helps for the Quiet Hour from the most eminent writers, like Murray, Meyer, Cuyler, Miller, Chapman, Moody, and many others.

Ques.—How can laboring men, who have to be at their work at seven o'clock in the morning, and perhaps walk two miles to get to it, keep the Quiet Hour? How can busy, tired mothers, who have little or no privacy, keep it?

Ans.—I have the fullest sympathy with these classes. My own labors are exhausting, and often keep me up until midnight or later, and the morning nap is sweet; but I have found the Quiet Hour invaluable, and I believe that there are very few who can not, if they will, get this quiet fifteen minutes, and none who will not find vast profit in it. It will mean fifteen minutes less sleep, but ten times fifteen minutes of refreshment and physical, mental, and spiritual tonic.

Ques.—What is the covenant of the Comrades of the Quiet Hour?

Ans.—*Trusting in the Lord Jesus Christ for strength, I will make it the rule of my life to set apart at least fifteen minutes every day, if possible in the early morning, for quiet meditation and direct communion with God.*

Ques.—How can I become a Comrade of the Quiet Hour?

Ans.—Send your name and address and the church to which you belong, with a stamp to cover postage, to Rev. Francis E. Clark, Tremont Temple, Boston, Mass., and your name will be enrolled and a covenant card will be duly sent you to sign and keep.

Will you not interest your friends in this most important movement, and send to the above address a list of those who desire to become "Comrades"?

Appendix VI

FACTS ABOUT THE TENTH LEGION OF THE UNITED SOCIETY OF CHRISTIAN ENDEAVOR

From a Leaflet by John Willis Baer.

Question.—"The Tenth Legion"—what is it?

Answer.—An *enrolment* of Christians whose practise it is to give to God for His work not less than one-tenth of their income.

Ques.—Who gave it the name?

Ans.—The New York City Christian Endeavor Union originated this tithe-givers' league.

Ques.—Where are the headquarters now?

Ans.—At the office of the United Society of Christian Endeavor, Tremont Temple, Boston, Mass.

Ques.—How did it come to be adopted by the United Society of Christian Endeavor?

Ans.—At the request of the New York Union. It never aspired to a national enrolment; and when the plan became known outside of New York, the demand for information became so extensive that the United Society, believing heartily in the "proportionate" giving to God, accepted the suggestion of W. L. Amerman, the originator of the plan, and early in the year 1897 commenced to promote the "Tenth Legion."

Ques.—What is the motto of the Tenth Legion?

Ans.—"Render unto God the things that are God's."

Ques.—Are any members enrolled that do not give as much as one-tenth of their income?

Ans.—No.

Ques.—How may we become enrolled as members of the Tenth Legion?

Ans.—Send a two-cent stamp and make application to John Willis Baer, Tremont Temple, Boston. A handsomely engraved certificate will then be mailed you.

Ques.—Are there any dues or taxes?

Ans.—None whatever.

Ques.—Is membership limited to Christian Endeavorers?

Ans.—No. Any one that gives God the *tithe* may join.

Ques.—Is not this idea of tithe-giving a narrow, legal, Jewish view of the whole question? Should we not consecrate the whole of our income rather than a small fraction?

Ans.—Every true tithe-giver does consecrate the whole of his property, but he also specifically gives *at least* one-tenth for the spread of the kingdom of God, while the

14   209

average gift of Christians for this purpose is not one-hundredth part of their income. This is a Christian vow, and is not a Jewish law simply because the Jews practised it. The Ten Commandments and the Sabbath belong to the Christian as well as to the Jew.

Ques.—Are members that have for years given God the *tithe* eligible to membership, or is the Tenth Legion organized for those that are beginners?

Ans.—It is for all that would like to be enrolled.

Ques.—What is the use of joining the Tenth Legion?

Ans.—To give this movement for generous giving the inspiration of numbers, and to enable you to push tithe-giving more forcibly yourself. As one tithe-giver of long standing says: "I have never before openly urged the practise for fear of seeming egotistical, but now I can urge the Tenth Legion."

Ques.—Can one withdraw at any time?

Ans.—Yes, and at the same time the certificate must be surrendered.

Ques.—Are the names of the members published?

Ans.—No. The enrolment is considered strictly confidential.

Ques.—Who is to decide what shall constitute the tenth of one's income?

Ans.—You yourself, with God, *conscientiously.*

Ques.—Who decides how to spend the money?

Ans.—The giver himself, and this becomes one of his greatest joys.

Ques.—Shall the net or the gross income be tithed?

Ans.—In the case of a salaried man, the gross income; in the case of a business man, the net income, after business expenses are deducted.

Ques.—What if one has no *fixed* income?

Ans.—Tithe whatever money comes to you.

Ques.—What if one is in debt?

Ans.—Our debt to God takes precedence of our debt to man. The latter must be paid, of course, and a tithe-giver will usually have more wherewith to pay his debts than if he had not given the tithe.

The Tenth Legion

Ques.—Is any part of the money to be given to the work of the United Society of Christian Endeavor?

Ans.—Not one penny. The United Society asks nothing for itself, and does not even receive voluntary contributions.

Ques.—Is it well to have a definite plan for spending the money?

Ans.—If you reserve something for the unexpected calls, yes. At the beginning of every year decide on a schedule of gifts to the mission boards of your denomination and to your church.

Ques.—Briefly, why should I recommend others to join the Tenth Legion?

Ans.—Because you received ten-tenths of your income from God, and should certainly return not less than one-tenth to His work.

Because tithe-giving does not prevent your giving more, if you have it to give.

Ques.—How may the claims of *The Tenth Legion* be brought before the Young People's society or the church?

Ans.—You may use the ballots sold by the United Society of Christian Endeavor for the purpose of finding out the present status of your members in this matter. Price, postpaid, fifteen cents a hundred. Get some tithe-giver to make an address. Have repeated the illustrated address on the Tenth Legion, by Amos R. Wells, sold by the United Society for $1.50 a hundred. Follow with a testimony meeting. Circulate the application blanks. Urge the matter personally. Appoint a Tenth-Legion committee to push the plan in all these ways.

Ques.—Where can leaflets be had that advocate the giving of not less than one-tenth to God?

Ans.—Address Layman, 310 Ashland Avenue, Chicago, Ill., and Publishing Department, United Society of Christian Endeavor, Boston, Mass.; also write to the missionary boards of your own denomination. Ask your pastor for the address of the latter. Send five cents with your request, to pay postage.

211

Training the Church of the Future

Ques.—Where can application blanks be obtained? *Ans.*—Slips like the following may be had of Secretary Baer, Tremont Temple, Boston, Mass. Price, ten cents a hundred.

"UNTO GOD THE THINGS THAT ARE GOD'S"

ENROLMENT BLANK.

Please enrol my name in

THE TENTH LEGION

of the United Society of Christian Endeavor as a Christian whose practise it is to give God the tithe, and send me the certificate of membership.

Name ....

Address... ....

Y. P. S. C. E. of ....*Church*

To JOHN WILLIS BAER,
   Tremont Temple, Boston, Mass.

(Send a two-cent stamp.)

If local or city union officers desire large quantities of this leaflet, they will be furnished for $1.50 a thousand, postpaid.

Appendix VII

THE MACEDONIAN PHALANX

By AMOS R. WELLS.

Ques.—What is the Macedonian Phalanx?
Ans.—It is an enrolment of those that give to the support of individual missionaries and mission workers.
Ques.—Can individuals join?

212

Ans.—Yes, if their individual gift is of the required amount.

Ques.—Who else can join?

Ans.—Any Christian Endeavor society whose gift fulfils the conditions.

Ques.—What kind of missionary worker must be supported, in whole or part?

Ans.—Any missionary on the home or foreign field, or a native preacher, teacher, Bible woman, or other Christian worker, or a student preparing for Christian work, or some definite and distinct part of mission work, as a hospital, free hospital bed, mission boat-building, church-planting, supporting Sunday-schools, and the like.

Ques.—How much money must be given?

Ans.—At least twenty dollars a year.

Ques.—Suppose the church is carrying on this work, and the individual or society contributes this amount to the church fund for the purpose?

Ans.—That meets all requirements for membership.

Ques.—Suppose the Christian Endeavor Society joins with the other societies of the same denomination for the same purpose, contributing at least twenty dollars?

Ans.—Each society so doing has a right to membership in the Phalanx.

Ques.—To whom are the contributions to be made?

Ans.—They are to be sent through the church to which the society or the individual belongs, and to the regular denominational missionary board.

Ques.—How often is the gift to be made?

Ans.—It is understood that the gift will be made once a year, and if for any reason the annual gift can not be made, the name should be withdrawn from membership.

Ques.—To whom are applications for membership to be sent?

Ans.—To John Willis Baer, general secretary of the United Society of Christian Endeavor, Tremont Temple, Boston, Mass.

Ques.—What is sent to the new member?

Ans.—A handsome lithographed certificate of membership, suitable for framing. It may be hung up in the society room as an incentive to missionary interest. At the same time the name is recorded on the books of the United Society of Christian Endeavor, and all items of general interest in regard to the new members are reported to the Endeavorers at large in the columns of *The Christian Endeavor World.*

Ques.—Is there any charge for enrolment?

Ans.—None; but ten cents is charged for the certificate, simply to cover the cost and postage.

Ques.—Are there any expenses connected with membership?

Ans.—None whatever, no dues or fees, and no obligations except those already defined, which relate to the annual gift.

Ques.—What is the purpose of the Macedonian Phalanx?

Ans.—To encourage a close connection between the giver and the missionary fields to which he is giving. It is believed that this is a decided stimulus to missionary zeal and generosity.

Ques.—How can this connection be promoted and utilized?

Ans.—By means of correspondence, by study of the particular field, by frequent reports to the society concerning it, by printing upon the society topic cards, calendars, year-books, and the like, the name of the missionary or the work supported, by displaying it prominently in the prayer-meeting room, by often talking over the work in the Christian Endeavor meeting, and praying for it.

Ques.—Does this support of a single worker diminish interest in other workers, and other fields and mission boards?

Ans.—No; it has been proved conclusively by the experience of many societies and churches that it does not.

Ques.—Has this movement the support of the missionary boards?

Ans.—It has their cordial indorsement. Indeed, several of them are maintaining workers for the very purpose of furthering some such movement as this.

Ques.—Who is to assign the worker to be supported?

Ans.—Enter into correspondence with the mission board whose work you wish to aid, and they will assign you a worker and put you in communication with him or her.

Ques.—What is hoped for from this movement?

Ans.—That it will make missions more real and vivid by personal contact with these men and women who are acting so nobly as our proxies, that it will increase our personal devotion to the cause, that it will enlarge our gifts greatly, add to the resources of the missionary boards and make their income more certain, render Christians more intelligent regarding the mission fields, make their prayers more fervent for the success of missions, and in every way help toward the accomplishment of the Great Commission.

Appendix VIII

THE CHRISTIAN ENDEAVOR CIVIC CLUB

By AMOS R. WELLS and FRANCIS E. CLARK.

For a long while Christian Endeavor has stood for Christian citizenship. Much has been done by individual societies and unions, but no *general concreted plan* has hitherto been proposed for making our abstract views on good citizenship concrete.

As long ago as 1893, at the Montreal convention, it was proposed and unanimously agreed that Christian citizenship should be one of the departments of Christian Endeavor as a movement, and in thousands of communities the thought has quickened the political conscience of young men, aroused them to a sense of their civic duty, and promoted most important reforms.

Training the Church of the Future

AN ADVANCE STEP.

But the time has come for a new and advance step along this line.

The murder of a beloved President by the red hand of an anarchist, the big Tammany in New York City and the little Tammanies that are smaller only because the towns are smaller, the colossal corruption in Philadelphia—all these evils call for the timely appeal of Dr. Capen, the vigorous address of the trustees of the United Society, and the practical constitution for "Christian Endeavor Civic Clubs" outlined by Professor Wells, and printed in another part of this appendix.

A CAMPAIGN OF INFORMATION.

The reason why corruption has been rampant in some of our cities is that the people have not been informed, have not taken pains to inform themselves of their own municipal affairs. How many of my readers know how they are governed; are acquainted with their city charter; know about their city's school system, its poor-laws, its streets and sewers, the municipal platforms of the parties and their political machinery?

The Civic Clubs will give just this information. They afford a chance for study as well as for discussion. They can go to the root of the matter. They may conduct a campaign of information in regard to most important matters that young citizens can study.

THE LYCEUM IDEA.

They will promote facility of public utterance and debate on the questions of the day. Dr. Capen says that young Irish-Americans are often better informed about measures of current politics, and better able to debate them, than young American-Americans, too many of whom are interested in everything but their own city or town.

216

The Civic Club

The young Irish-Americans ought to have the influence and the offices if they have political information and alertness in discussion. They will get them and keep them.

The old-fashioned lyceum was a splendid practical school for debate and information for many a country boy.

The C. E. C. C. (Christian Endeavor Civic Club) may bring back the palmy days of the old lyceum in country and city, and apply this greatly neglected force to the regeneration of our political life.

VILLAGE IMPROVEMENT.

In village improvement the Civic Club may be most useful. There is not a village in the United States or Canada, beautiful as many of them are, that may not be improved by intelligent study of the situation and energetic action, consulting, of course, older friends and enlisting them in any proposed plans.

Many villages already have Improvement Societies, which in every case, I believe, would rejoice in the interest and cooperation of a Civic Club of young people.

. . . . .

In fact, the vistas of usefulness that open up before such a club are almost endless. A careful study of the proposed constitution printed in this appendix will reveal many of them, and a good manual of practical work is Professor Wells's little book entitled "Citizens in Training."

Let me ask every reader to consider whether there is not room for a Civic Club in his local Christian Endeavor union, if not in his society.

Count well the cost in time and energy, so that it may not be a short-lived failure, and then "go in to win"—to win a better nation, a better city, or a better village through the Christian Endeavor Civic Club.

217

CONSTITUTION

PROPOSED FOR THE CHRISTIAN ENDEAVOR CIVIC
CLUBS.

ARTICLE I.—*Name.*

This organization shall be called the Christian Endeavor Civic Club, Number..... (The number of the charter issued by the United Society of Christian Endeavor. If desired, the club may be called a Christian Endeavor Congress, following the organization and methods of our national Congress or legislatures, the members choosing imaginary constituencies, bringing in bills, presenting resolves, and conducting all the work of the organization on legislative models.)

ARTICLE II.—*Object.*

The object of the Christian Endeavor Civic Club shall be the promotion of a better citizenship, through the study of civic problems, through training in debate and parliamentary practise, and through such active participation in public affairs as may be practicable and proper.

ARTICLE III.—*Motto.*

The motto of the Civic Club shall be Virgil's words, "The noblest motive is the public good."

ARTICLE IV.—*Officers.*

Its officers shall be a president, a vice-president, a secretary, and a treasurer, whose duties shall be those usually assigned to such officers. They shall be elected annually, at the first meeting in..........., one nomination for each office being made through a nominating committee appointed by the club two weeks before the date of election.

ARTICLE V.—*The Executive Committee.*

The general conduct of the club shall be in the hands of its officers, acting in conjunction with an executive

218

The Civic Club

committee of five. This executive committee shall consist of Christian Endeavorers, and shall be the connecting link between the club and the Christian Endeavor union (or society, if the club is formed under the auspices of a single society). It shall report to the union at its business meetings, and it shall present to the club all candidates for membership, making an earnest endeavor to obtain for the club all suitable persons.

ARTICLE VI.—*Membership.*

Membership in the club shall be open to all young men of good character who may be recommended by the executive committee and elected by the club. They shall become members on signing this constitution.

ARTICLE VII.—*Meetings.*

The club shall meet on the first and third Monday evenings of each month. (Of course any week-day evening may be chosen, and the meetings may be held only once a month. The summer meetings may be omitted.) The following order shall usually be followed:

1. Opening prayer.
2. Reading of the minutes.
3. Unfinished business.
4. Reports of committees.
5. New business.
6. Reports on current events, with discussion.
7. Study of civics, or
   Address, followed by discussion, or
   Debate, or
   Report of committees of inquiry, followed by discussion.
8. Announcements.
9. Adjournment.

ARTICLE VIII.—*Visitors.*

Members of the club may invite their gentleman friends to visit the club at any time. Occasional meetings shall be set apart as ladies' nights, when each member will be at liberty to invite his lady friends. By vote of the club, occasional public meetings may be held.

ARTICLE IX.—*Standing Committees.*

The following standing committees shall be elected, at the same time as the officers, in the same manner, and to serve for a year. Each shall consist of three persons, the one named first to serve as chairman.

1. *Program Committee.* This committee shall arrange programs for the meetings, obtaining speakers, selecting subjects for debate, outlining courses of study, and planning whatever additional features it can devise. All its proposals must be presented to the club, for suggestions and formal approval.

2. *Publicity Committee.* It shall be the duty of this committee to make known, through the press and in other ways, the work of the club, publishing its conclusions, and seeking to arouse interest in its meetings through posters and other advertisements.

3. *Village Improvement Committee.* This committee shall study the condition of the community, and shall make suggestions for the material and social welfare of the town, first submitting to the club all its proposals. (A large work is before this committee in many places beautifying the streets, establishing drinking-fountains, planting trees, founding town libraries, arranging lecture courses, and the like. Of course, ordinarily, their work can be done only by interesting in their plans the more powerful advocacy of older citizens.)

(Other committees may be added.)

ARTICLE X.—*Committees of Inquiry.*

From time to time the club may appoint committees of inquiry, large or small as it chooses, whose duty it will be to make special studies of the phase of civics assigned to them, presenting reports to the club as their work proceeds, and suggesting to the program committee speakers familiar with the subject given them to study, and also topics for debate and discussion along the line of their inquiry. (For example, such committees might be formed to study and report on the public schools, the streets and roads, temperance laws, building laws, fire department, police department, public charities, prisons, courts, elections, party organization, caucuses, city and county organization, State legislature, post-offices, newspapers, railroads, water-supply, Sabbath-observance, asylums, public records, board of health, public library, taxes. Public officials and others most intimately acquainted with these themes should be invited to address the club upon them, replying at the close to any questions the club may ask,—such officials, for example, as street commissioners, members of the school board, health officers, public register, selectman, assessor, councilman, postmaster, water commissioner, judge of election, prison warden, building inspector, public librarian.) Conclusions regarding these topics may be formulated by the club and published.

ARTICLE XI.—*Civic Action.*

The club will not refrain from practical participation in public affairs, provided always it strictly refuses to take partizan action. For example, it may, for the guidance of its members, obtain information concerning the records of candidates, but it will pass no vote indorsing any candidate. It may petition and work for the enactment of ordinances and statutes, but will not ally itself with any political party.

ARTICLE XII. —*Civic Studies.*

The club may engage in the study of civics, either through a text-book, under a leader, or through a course of lectures. The reading and discussion of books and articles on civic and patriotic themes shall form a portion of its work. This study may be carried on at home, and the results presented before the club in the form of essays, abstracts, talks, or discussions.

ARTICLE XIII.—*Current Events.*

It will be one purpose of the club to keep its members intelligent regarding the progress of the world's history. To that end, reporters from the leading nations and regions of the earth may be appointed, whose duty it will be to become thoroughly informed concerning current events in their respective fields, ready to report them at any meeting, and answer questions concerning them. These members may be called "Reporter for Germany," "Reporter for the Southern States," "Reporter for India," etc.

ARTICLE XIV.—*Amendment.*

This Constitution may be amended by a three-fourths vote of the members present at any meeting, provided notice of the proposed amendment has been given at a meeting of the club two weeks in advance.

(This Constitution is proposed merely as an outline for the guidance of the clubs, who will form their own constitutions to meet the local needs and circumstances. Many of the minor points here included might well be relegated to a set of by-laws. It would be best to start with a constitution as simple as possible, letting its growth be a matter of experience.)

Appendix IX

THE CHRISTIAN ENDEAVOR HOME CIRCLE
By FRANCIS E. CLARK, D.D.

The time has come, I believe, to make definite and more emphatic the advance step that was proposed three years ago at Nashville and emphasized again at the Cincinnati convention—the matter of Religion in the Home, especially as centering about family worship.

Family religion is a foundation-stone of all our religious life in church and state, and family worship lies

222

near the foundation of all family religion. In building the family altar, religion builds itself up.

Tho household prayers are not by any means the sum of family religion, or even its beginning; still they are an expression of it—definite and genuine expression, which has sadly fallen into disuse, and which Christian Endeavor can most properly do its utmost to revive.

NATURAL EFFORT FOR CHRISTIAN ENDEAVORERS.

It is not a forced and unnatural thing for Christian Endeavor to stand for family religion; not a trick to add something new, but a natural, legitimate development of the Christian Endeavor movement.

There are tens of thousands of families now where one or both of the heads of the household are or have been active members of the Society. If Christian Endeavor means anything to them, it means that they will carry their religion into their new-made homes. But there are others besides husbands and wives who control the destinies of the home. The children, the brothers and sisters, the unmarried aunts, all have responsibilities for establishing and maintaining home religion; and in many homes they can, if they will, have family prayers. It is as natural that Christian Endeavor should stand for Christian family life as for Christian citizenship for Christian missions.

WHO SECONDS THE MOTION?

Who will second this new effort of Christian Endeavor? I want to hear about ten thousand seconds; and, to make the matter very definite, I propose that those who will form themselves into A HOME CIRCLE OF CHRISTIAN ENDEAVOR join an enrolment that requires no officers, meetings, or constitution, but a simple agreement like the one on the following page.

This covenant, you will notice, is simple, short, and definite, and yet it leaves much to the individual, and does not tie him down with unnecessary rules.

Christian Endeavor Home Circle.

TRUSTING in the Lord Jesus Christ for strength, we will endeavor to maintain Family Worship in our home, and will strive to make it, through kindness, courtesy, and mutual helpfulness, a household of God.

Signed......................................

....

A FLEXIBLE PROPOSAL.

The family can maintain morning worship or evening worship or both. Even those who are so scattered that they can come together for household prayer only once a week can enter this Home Circle, tho it is understood that *daily* family prayer is generally meant.

The exercise may be longer or shorter. It may take three minutes or fifteen. The father may conduct it alone, or father and mother and all the children may join in it, and this would often be better still.

The prayers may be extemporaneous or written. In fact, there is the utmost variety possible, but at the same time there is this strong bond of unity that as households we who are enrolled shall bow reverently before our Father in heaven and crave His blessing on our home through Jesus Christ our Lord.

Few earnest Christian Endeavorers need be left out of this circle. If one is only in a subordinate position in the home, the idea can be carried out. If parents are indifferent, gather the little brothers and sisters for worship. At least once a week in almost every home there could be family Bible-reading and prayer if only one member of the household were inclined to conduct it.

THE VAST POSSIBILITIES OF THIS EFFORT.

The possibilities for good of this effort are almost unbounded. It may do not a little toward stemming the

224

tide of irreligion in the family. It may help to sweeten and refine family life for generations to come. It may increase the love of parents and children and brothers and sisters. It may help to establish in many households reverence for divine things, familiarity with the Word of God, and devotion to the highest ideals.

It may result in raising up ministers of the Gospel, and missionaries, and Christian workers whose lips were first touched with a live coal from off the family altar.

All these blessed results and many more are more than possible, and are certain to result from a wide revival of interest in and practise of household religion. For those who can not at first trust themselves to extemporaneous prayer in the family circle, there are various manuals of devotion.

SET AN EXAMPLE BY ENROLING YOUR OWN NAME.

Let all who wish to join the *Christian Endeavor Home Circle* send in their names at once. Even if for many years you have practised family worship, send in your names for the benefit of others who may be led by your example to begin. Let the theme be considered in Christian Endeavor conventions and union meetings, and let all who believe in the plan try to induce others to enrol. No obligations are assumed beyond the very simple ones involved in the covenant printed above.

Cards containing the covenant, with blank spaces for all members of the family to sign, will be forwarded on receipt of a stamp for postage, and engraved certificates suitable for framing will soon be furnished for ten cents, which will not more than cover the cost.

Fellow Endeavorers and Christian friends, let us heartily enter into this plan, which may bring such untold blessings to our individual life, our home life, our national life; and let us take for our motto, "*As for me and my house, we will serve the Lord.*"

Young People's
Prayer - Meetings:

HOW TO CONDUCT THEM

A BOOK FOR SOCIETIES OF CHRISTIAN ENDEAVOR
AND FOR ALL OTHER ORGANIZATIONS FOR
THE DEVELOPMENT OF THE CHRISTIAN
CHARACTER OF YOUNG CONVERTS

Valuable manuals concerning the conduct of the general prayer-meeting are numerous, but comparatively little has been written regarding its smaller brother—the " *Young People's* Prayer-meeting," The recent rapid growth of religious organizations for Young People make such a work as this very desirable and valuable. These chapters are the outgrowth of experience and personal effort. The plans suggested have all been successfully tried. The author has given the results of a very wide and long experience, and is, therefore, first of all, *practical* in his suggestions. The topics given have been *selected* with care from thousands of lists prepared by or for young people. The book is one of great importance in the conduct of the Young People's Meetings. Pastors would do well to secure the volume, if for no other purpose than to loan or give it to those in whose behalf the meetings are held.

" This is a good book, and contains many valuable suggestions in regard to the best method of conducting prayer-meetings, especially for young people."— **Methodist Recorder**, Pittsburg.

" It it a capital book. Every pastor who reads it will find in it some hints of decided value. The topics are treated in a sensible and altogether practical manner. We heartily commend the book not to pastors alone, but to all who are interested in this matter."—**The Advance**, Chicago.

" It is an unusual combination of Christian common sense, with a broad and also a minute knowledge of the needs, desires, tasts, and feelings of young people. The training of young converts, and the making of them before they are trained, the place and work of the young people's meeting, the best methods of conducting it, and its relation to the development and power of the Church— these, under various heads, are considered fully and wisely. . . . We commend it heartily. It is especially indispensable."—**The Congregationalist**, Boston.

" It is full of helpful suggestions in regard to the training and education of young Christians, and the conduct of young people's meetings. The chapters devoted to an account of the Society of Christian Endeavor will repay perusal. We take pleasure in recommending the book to all Christians."—**Christian Advocate**, Buffalo.

" This is an excellent manual. . . . The teachings of this volume upon the training of young converts, the importance of an early formed habit of working in social services, and the best modes of awakening their interest in them, are every way excellent, and full of valuable suggestions. The large collection of prayer-meeting topics, also, will be found very serviceable."—**Zion's Herald**, Boston.

" The author is an authority upon the question he has undertaken to discuss Few men in this country or elsewhere have given the subject of the religious culture of young people more earnest and solicitous attention. The book is full of hints that can easily be reduced to practise. And this is why the book will prove valuable."—**Michigan Christian Advocate**, Detroit.

Cloth, 12mo, 167 pp.   Price, 75 cents, post-free.

FUNK & WAGNALLS COMPANY
30 Lafayette Place, New York